Followship:

Pastoring In His Presence

Jim Cobrae

Followship: Pastoring In His Presence
ISBN: 978-1-939570-86-4
Copyright © 2018 by Jim Cobrae

Published by Word and Spirit Publishing
P.O. Box 701403
Tulsa, Oklahoma 74170
wordandspiritpublishing.com

DEDICATION

I would like to take the time to dedicate this writing to the most important people in my life, who have shaped my heart though their love, hope, and faith—not only in God, but also in me. Without this godly family serving our King, who knows where we would have ended up?

I first dedicate this work to my amazing wife who for the last forty years has been my living, breathing, walking concordance and is my very best friend. I also dedicate this writing to my children, all in the service of the King, and I want to thank them in the order they were born. My daughter Miranda pastors with her husband Hennie Bosman in Temecula, California. Both are some of the greatest ministers I've ever known and the best parents to their four sons. Look out next generations! My daughter, Kimberlee, is my hero because she is raising three more grandsons—by herself. She is known for her serving, and I love her. Jessica Joy and her husband Daniel J. Roth are now the lead pastors of our church—The Rock Church and World Outreach Center. Both young, yet God has greatly advanced them with godly wisdom and ministry giftings. They are parents to two more grandsons and our first grand daughter. My youngest son Luke and his wonderful wife Stacey have two more of our grandchildren. They are just starting the great adventure of pioneering their own church. God has imbued them with talent and gifts far beyond anything I could have ever imagined, and the Gospel will be preached to the next generations.

I also want to mention my wonderful spiritual son and daughter, Eddie and Dawna Elguera, who pastor The Rock Church in Coachella Valley. They are so faithful and such a blessing! Last but not least, I want to thank my friend Mark Horan and his wife Joy, who live in Australia, for the calls of encouragement every week. Mark's gift is encouragement—he's truly a modern day Barnabas. Whoever has Mark around them is a truly blessed person!

TABLE OF CONTENTS

Acknowledgements

I'd like to thank my publisher, Keith Provance and his team at Word and Spirit, and my editor, Joshua Lease at Aegis Editing, for believing in the word God gave me to share and for helping to make this book a blessing to everyone it reaches. I believe pastors everywhere will benefit from my successes and failures because these people and many others came alongside to help me share God's message with them.

Introduction

It is with the greatest caution and apprehension that I write any suggestions or share with pastors anything about how to get their churches to grow. Growth is the strongest desire found in a pastor's heart for his church; it is a passion given and placed by God. That is why almost all pastors fervently desire church growth.

Therein lies the problem—a problem that sits in the "heart." Over the years, I have found it is a heart that doesn't always want to listen to very much of what others have to say, especially if it comes off as brash or arrogant. So for years I have kept my thoughts to myself and just practiced church growth principles in my own church.

Times have changed, and so have I. I am now in my seventies and have been a senior pastor and teacher for around forty years. What started out as an experiment turned out to be one of the greatest blessings of my life. I have learned a lot over these years and openly admit I would love to share what God taught me with someone who wants to learn. You see, I have pastored everything from small, barely-getting-by churches to one of the largest and greatest churches in America.

I hope you don't think I'm bragging about our church; as you will see if you keep reading, I've learned my lesson about bragging! However, in order for you to listen to what I have to say, I need to communicate in terms that will attract your interest. For example, if I told you I had a church of twenty-five people and I was going to speak to you about church growth, you would stop reading right now. However, when I tell you that in twenty-five years our church, The Rock Church and World Outreach Center, went from twelve people to almost 24,000 members and about 18,000 in weekly attendance, that might attract you! In addition, the Lord used two of the most unlikely people the world has ever known in my wife Deby and me. Here is my point: if God can use Deby and me, how much more can our great God use you?

By the way, it is not just "your" desire for your church to grow—it is God's too! He would not have placed that desire in your heart unless there could be godly growth. He has a plan and never gives us an assignment without the ability to get it done. So, then, the million-dollar question is, "Why doesn't my church grow?"

As you read, you may be challenged and frustrated with my "in-your-face" personality. I have never described myself as a gentle person, and making changes and doing some things God has shown me may be a difficult task, because they may require doing something different than you have done it before.

But before we get into the heart of this matter of growing our churches, I want to tell you how it all began so you can understand just how far the Lord has taken us. Allow me to go back to our beginnings, about forty years.

Let Me Introduce Myself

This road of faith starts, as always, with multiple choices for direction. I was a young man of thirty-two with three failed marriages and a futile effort in professional baseball. I had married the same woman twice, and wife number two left me after sixty days of marriage with no explanation. I came home from work one day, noticed sawdust by the front door, and quickly discovered all the locks were changed and a letter was taped to the front door from her attorney!

Since Deby was going to be wife number three and marriage number four, I was determined not to make a mess out of my life again. Before you read about the wonderful things the Lord has done for us, I need to explain just how hurt and messed up we both were so you can see our brokenness before we married.

I was recovering from the hurt and rejection of being divorced multiple times and my failed professional baseball career. I knew my life needed radical change, so I chose to draw close to the Lord and commit exclusively to Him. I was living in Santa Barbara, California, and looking for a local church that would accept me after three divorces (which in itself was very difficult). I focused on growing in His Word and developing my business, and I swore off all relationships with the opposite sex. I was content faithfully serving God and watching my business prosper; I was not looking for a relationship and definitely not a wife. But God had other plans!

The church I began attending had just started a "house ministry" for those who wanted to be discipled. It was the seventies; the Jesus Movement was sweeping through California as the Holy Spirit used a great man of God to begin a counter-revolution of love in Jesus Christ. At that time, the churches were traditional in music and doctrine, but the Lord was revealing just how much He loved the messed up youth of my generation.

This unique work was a new church meeting at the YMCA and full of young people brimming over with hope. My future wife, Deby, received a gift certificate to attend a new yoga class at the YMCA, and instead of yoga, she discovered this church. On her way out of the building, she saw a closed door with a window, and when she peeked in, it was full of people her age lifting up their hands and singing with someone leading them with a guitar! Remember, it was the seventies—churches didn't have guitars or drums. And who ever heard of a church at the YMCA? She skipped her yoga class and went into that room, and the rest is history. God got ahold of her, set her heart on fire, and she fell head-over-heels in love with Jesus. She immediately gave her heart to the Lord and was convicted by the Holy Spirit about her lifestyle. Knowing she had to make some drastic changes, she found herself with no place to live or to raise her eight-year-old daughter.

The young pastor of the church and his wife took personal hold of her need, rented a large Victorian home, and invited my future wife and six others to live with them and become disciples of Jesus Christ. Having the opportunity to learn and grow in the Lord was life-changing in every way.

So, to cut to the headlines, there was no doubt my future wife was coming back from a very backslidden life; she was divorced with one precious little girl (my Miranda) and was delivered from a lifestyle that included drugs, sex, and some exceptionally wrong choices. And since there was no doubt I had also made some critically wrong decisions and had experienced great disappointment, our young pastors, being the wonderful couple they were, felt we may be perfect for each other and should meet.

That first meeting began a life-long love affair, and nine months later I took my new bride on the honeymoon of her life. Forget Hawaii or any other romantic spot—I was so hungry to know God, I took my bride to a "faith convention" where we could hear the Word of God! Every one of our family and friends thought we were crazy. We very likely were, but that was okay with us! I knew if we were to make it in this marriage, it would only be successful because of living in His presence and doing His will in our lives.

Forty years later, here we are: four kids (hers, mine, and ours), twelve grandchildren, and one great grandchild. God has filled our hearts and every area of our lives with His favor and blessing. All of our family is serving the Lord, and we stand as a living memorial to reveal what God can do with one messed-up couple who wants to please Him more than ourselves.

> From His pleasure comes His presence, from His presence comes His anointing, and from His anointing comes His direction

I have discovered when I live my life to please Him, I live in His pleasure, where everything we need is found! He opened my eyes to see that from God's pleasure comes His presence, from His presence comes His anointing, and from His anointing comes His direction. I can tell you as an old man that living by His direction and dwelling in His presence will bring more fulfillment and satisfaction than anything this world can offer.

As you read on, in order for you to see the things that I have learned and understand what it is that I am saying, there must be some common ground for our mutual understanding. Let me explain in the first chapter.

Chapter 1

Leadership Is Followship

When Deby and I realized that the only One who truly deserves to be followed is the same One who cannot fail, then and only then did we realize that true Christian leadership is simply being one who follows Him. Exclusively following Him will lead you, and all others, to the greatest fulfillment life can offer. Massive church growth will follow, so let me explain real leadership—what I call "followship."

Leadership is not the ability to lead people somewhere but the ability to follow Someone (Jesus) who has already been there. Although this thinking may seem to conflict with modern-day leadership trends where everything is based on the "new and changing" culture and church, the ability to *follow* Him makes great leaders, and without this, there can be no true or real leadership.

Isn't it true that we are to be followers of Jesus? Jesus does not follow *me*—I must learn to follow *Him*. This is where real true leadership begins, and church growth follows.

Followship

I know what you are thinking, and you are right—there is no such word as "followship" in the dictionary. But there should be! Since I have created this word, here is my definition: "the passion and capacity to set yourself aside and follow the true and only leader, Jesus Christ." I believe He stated it something like this: "Pick up your cross and follow me."

> Followship is the adventure of finding your real leadership ability by following God.

Followship is the adventure of finding your real leadership ability by following God.

As a Christian who is completely committed to following the Word of God, I personally have a hard time accepting any lessons about the church from the world's view of success. I feel that humanity's true "right and wrong" or "good and bad" is largely determined by how the world views success, which is often based on results such as money and numbers. Under this model, church growth would look something like this: More people generally equate to more resources, and that will translate to more money, which will then bring success. That cannot be the goal of the Kingdom!

If money and numbers of people equate to spirituality, then Las Vegas, having both in abundance, should be the most spiritual city in America! Obviously, that is not the kind of example God wants His people to follow, yet our leadership practices often times accept the ways of accumulation that the world uses. What works in the world's system should not be the compass for our directions in the Kingdom of God.

I have found that as I listen to today's experts on leadership, it appears many have derived their advice and counsel from what the business world is achieving. In doing so, it can be very easy to exalt the efforts of people above the efforts of God…and not even know you are doing so! We can frustrate the grace of God and end up disappointing Him when we are actually trying our best to please Him!

Following the successful tips of the prosperous and profitable is an easy road to find. Many well-known leaders in the church have taken these successful business principles and put them into familiar vocabulary that serious and determined Christian leaders can relate to. But is that the only path to church growth? No. I believe God has a better way.

Follow the King

Ok, you may say, "Not a bad idea; it is working for them," but does this kind of leadership apply to the church of the Living God? Coming out of the business world into the world of pastoring, I asked this big question myself. I knew these principles backward and forward. I had built a highly successful business and was experiencing a great deal of prosperity. I had read every book I could get my hands on, had gone to seminars, and even became a top spokesman in my own company. But that is when I learned what is right to man is not always right with God!

When I stepped out of the marketplace and into the pastures of God, I discovered God's church has completely different bottom lines and different marching orders. I realized I could operate based on worldly results, and that could bring me a measure of success. But ultimately the question was, "Did it bring God's plan to pass, and did it make *Him* happy?" I struggled with the answer, finally coming to the truth that the answer was, in fact, *no!*

Even though many will write best-selling books about what the world is doing and put it in Christian terms, it does not make them experts on Christian leadership, which should actually be "followship." I don't want to sound unkind or critical, nor am I anyone's judge. I know some effort is better than no effort, so I can say a big "thank you" for those who have labored to enhance the skills of others so that they may approach higher ground.

I realize that their motives and advice are both sincere and direct, but what if there is another way—a way that is not necessarily easy or obvious but is understandable? What if God's absolute will for you is to find His best and be successful in the church you are pastoring—but His plan may not be what you expect or desire? I am writing this book to bring a completely different approach to the word "leadership," which is to show you how I learned to follow and develop "followship."

I believe that godly leadership is better described as "followship," meaning that true leadership in the kingdom of God is about how best to follow the King. Jesus modeled this continually with His words and actions. He told His disciples that when they saw Him, they saw the Father and that the words that He spoke were not His but the Father's (John 14:7-10). He and the Father were so close they were as one carrying out the Father's plan by the power of the Holy Spirit.

> True leadership in the kingdom of God is about how best to follow the King.

Do you believe that could be done with a person? A pastor? I do—maybe not to the perfection that Jesus carried it out with the Father, but for some who see it and really want it, "all things are possible."

Therefore, my first lesson in followship was learning to follow God and not people. But that was just the beginning; I had to learn from His plan what was good for me and what was not. He redefined my definition of good and evil, and it began to give me new revelation in truly hearing His voice.

For someone who had never pastored and now found himself pastoring his own church, I needed to learn God's opinion and direction, not someone else's. The countless pastors' conferences I attended were helpful, but I still found myself asking God what He wanted me to do. Here is what I learned first—the definition of "good."

Chapter 2

What Is Good?

In order for us to proceed, we must learn the definition of one simple little word—"good." What is good?

A rich young ruler had come to the Lord and asked Him a question. The statement from this ruler and the reply from Jesus deserve some real attention because it is a very important revelation.

> Now behold, one came and said to Him, "**Good Teacher,** what **good thing shall I do that I may have eternal life?**" So He said to him, "**Why do you call Me good? No one is good but One, that is, God.** But if you want to enter into life, keep the commandments.
>
> Matthew 19:16-17

The ruler addresses Jesus as "**good teacher**." Jesus does not comment on the word "teacher" but calls attention to the word "**good**." He replies that no one is good but God. I believe Jesus was saying something very profound to all of us and using this man's statement as an example for us to learn.

No one is good but God. If that is true, then what God says is good and what the world says is "good" are often times very, very different.

In order to further understand, let's go back to the very beginning, where we see Adam and Eve in Genesis 2.

*And the LORD God formed man of the dust of the ground, and breathed into his nostrils the breath of life; and man became a living being. The LORD God planted a garden eastward in Eden, and there He put the man whom He had formed. And out of the ground the LORD God made every tree grow that is pleasant to the sight and good for food. The tree of life was also in the midst of the garden, **and the tree of the knowledge of good and evil.***

Genesis 2:7-9

Please note that I highlighted the words, **"And the tree of the knowledge of good and of evil."** (I will be highlighting phrases and words in many of the Scriptures in this book.) Let's look on.

*Then the LORD God took the man and put him in the garden of Eden to tend and keep it. And the LORD God commanded the man, saying, "Of every tree of the garden you may freely eat; **but of the tree of the knowledge of good and evil you shall not eat**, for in the day that you eat of it you shall surely die." And the LORD God said, "It is not good that man should be alone; I will make him a helper comparable to him."*

Genesis 2:15-18

Note the words, **"The tree of the knowledge of good and of evil you shall not eat."**

What is "the tree of the knowledge of good and evil?" It would appear that if anyone eats the fruit from this tree, it would give them the ability to determine for themselves what is "good" or what is "evil."

Before Adam and Eve ate the fruit, *God* determined what was good and evil in their world. God brought them to the good in everything and warned them of all evil. They just needed to follow Him (they were to be the original "followshippers").

So before they ate from the tree, God directed everything they knew and did. What was good and what was evil came directly from God. However, from the moment they ate, Adam and Eve now decided for *themselves* what was good to them and what was evil for them. They were no longer dependent on God, His insight, or His will for them (we will look at this word "dependent" in more detail later in the book, so take note of it).

When Adam and Eve ate the fruit of the tree of the knowledge of good and evil, they separated themselves from God and began determining their own choices of good and evil. They lost God's "good" and replaced it with their own.

God told them that the moment they ate from that tree, they would die. That is exactly what happened. They died, for that actually is what the definition of death is—separation. They separated from the Godhead and died spiritually.

Look what happened to them: their eyes were opened, and they immediately knew *apart from God* that they were "naked." They hid themselves from His presence, tried to cover up their nakedness, and entered into fear.

For God knows that in the day you eat of it your eyes will be opened, and you will be like God, knowing good and evil." So when the woman saw that the tree was good for food, that it was pleasant to the eyes, and a tree desirable to make one wise, she took of its fruit and ate. She also gave to her husband with her, and he ate. Then the eyes of both of them were opened, and they knew that they were naked; and they sewed fig leaves together and made themselves coverings. And they heard the sound of the LORD God walking in the garden in the cool of the day, and Adam and his wife hid themselves from the presence of the LORD God among the trees of the garden. Then the LORD God called to Adam and said to him, "Where are you?" So he said, "I heard Your voice in the garden, and I was afraid because I was naked; and I hid myself."

Genesis 3:5-10

In a way, Satan was right when he told the woman she would be "like God," knowing good and evil. The only problem was she was *not* God, and the good and evil they were going to discover was now based on their own ability and understanding and not what God said! Their take on "good" or "evil" was not God's! They thought they did not need God to tell them what life was all about because they could now figure it out for themselves. This is why the world is such a mess and continues to be a mess.

> Man does not even know what is good or what is evil.

Let's go back to Jesus. When the ruler says, "**good teacher**," Jesus takes the opportunity to call attention to the fact that man does not even know what is good or what is evil. Since the fall of man, we have failed to listen to God for directions and can now determine our own way—what is good and what is evil, independent from God—all based on our own personal **knowledge** and **feelings.**

Understanding this: for me to take my leadership ideas from the business world would make me a very foolish followshipper because the root of that comes from the tree of the knowledge of good and evil and cannot and will not produce a work that will be pleasing to God. It would be impossible to please Him, because God never designed us to figure out life *our way* but to live life *His way.*

The world celebrates accomplishment, accumulation, and personal giftings. However, God only celebrates these when they are directed and empowered by Him. Only a back-to-the-Garden relationship will do. Can you even imagine God being thrilled over someone's personal accomplishment that is void of His directions and His empowerment? That would be like God declaring that man can make it without Him and will not die, and that would make God a liar and the serpent truthful. It will never happen.

Bad Decisions, Bad Directions

Let us go back to Genesis 3. Just a few verses after they ate from the tree, the first thing that they did was to make bad decisions, which gave them bad directions. Remember, they hid from God's presence and were afraid. One chapter later, their child becomes a murderer by killing his brother because one followed God and the other followed what *he* thought was good. Again, we see failure because our choices are not God's choices, and even though they may seem and feel right, they can be very wrong!

Only God is good, and only God can determine what is truly evil. Good is God's will, God's way. Anything that is not God's will done in God's way fails to live up to the standard of what God would call "good."

The word "evil" is being separated from good. Case in point, Cain and Abel brought sacrifices. Cain brought his sacrifice from the earth, which was cursed; Abel, from his flock by faith (Heb. 11:4). Since faith comes by hearing God's Word, we know God told them what to bring to give Abel faith to bring it. Abel's sacrifice was accepted, Cain's rejected. As a result, Cain rose up and killed his brother after God warned him that sin was crouching at the door and he must not give in (Gen. 4:7).

Moses gives us another example of following God's directions but not doing it His way. When God told him to speak to the rock and not the people, he followed his own way, struck the rock and spoke to the children of Israel. As a result, he was not able to enter into the Promised Land and was only allowed to see it from afar (Num. 20:12, 27:14).

The Word of God is full of examples of people doing God's will our own way, or doing our own will our way! How much more successful would we be if we could just understand God created us to hear His voice, do as He says, and follow Him!

> Good is God's will, God's way. Simple, but not always easy.

Every time I want you to remember this concept about the word good, I will put it in quotation marks—"**good**." Remember, Jesus said God alone is good. He has a good plan for us. If we simply hear and do what He says, it will work. **Good is God's will, God's way. Simple, but not always easy.**

To review: our leadership should actually be "followship." We must get back to what God says is good and evil, right and wrong, and simply follow Him. If we follow God, how can we miss as we build our churches?

If you agree, then welcome to the bizarre world of followship—a world of amazing peace, overwhelming comfort, and rest. It is a world of assurance, fulfillment, and untold blessings, because it involves doing what God calls "good."

Chapter 3

Living to Become Effective

People can hear from God to do service for Him, but *how* to do this is a completely different thing. It may be just my opinion, but I think many pastors may not honestly understand what they are doing and why they are doing it. At least I know I didn't! This is one of the main reasons I wrote this book. I had to learn so much the hard way, and whatever success I have had, I want to pass it on to those who could use what I have to share.

I find it interesting that when there is an impression that God wants to do something in someone's life, the first thought is to become a pastor. Could this be because the office of the pastor is sometimes the only paid position in the church? Who knows?

What I do know is that knowing what to do can be very confusing and unclear. Somehow, inside of many of us is a feeling that we are to do something for God. However, the big question here is, "Is what you are doing the *right* thing for you to do?" Many do not sincerely know what they are to do and why they are to do it! That was definitely my experience. It seemed like I found myself groping for direction in the dark.

How can your work be successful if you do not know *why* you are doing what you are doing or even *how* to do it? In the business world, the goals and directions are clear, but God's Kingdom business is very different, and the learning curve is challenging. Over the years, I have found only a few who were willing to admit that they seemed to be in the dark about ministry. That means either I am abnormal or we pastors and leaders don't openly admit our confusion. How frustrating it is to be in that spot! I have seen so many good leaders and pastors who are just not sure about what they are doing and why they are doing it.

The Blind Leading the Blind

Here is my take on what happens. We pastors check out what someone else is doing that seems to be working and try to duplicate it in our own church. We just keep copying each other. We think that if it worked so well for others, it should work for us. However, here is the problem with that: We have to ask, "Did God tell me to do it that way?" If the answer is dubious, then we may have been getting our directions from some source *other than God.*

We all know that what works well for some people does not always work well for others. I can do the same thing the same way as another pastor and get completely different results. Why is that? Maybe it's a different city, different times, or, more importantly, maybe God just didn't want you to do it.

Let's get honest—God backs what He is involved in, and His favor and anointing are evident. The anointing may be on one church to be a certain way but may not be on another that operates in the same manner. They are different churches with different sets of skills and needs—and, most importantly, different assignments.

What worked for a church or even a business fifty years ago probably won't work today. The principles may be the same, but the methods, styles, and skills have all drastically changed. The God who created the Heavens and the Earth is a very creative God who can give us fresh ideas and strategies for our times and seasons. Stale and old ideas must change to keep up with the call that God has for us.

Please note that the *Gospel* never changes, but the method on how we implement our church services must change. I believe the directions on how we make those changes must come from God.

However, if you don't know who you are and what you are supposed to be doing, how can God get behind it? If you do not know what direction to take the church, then where will you end up? In addition, how can you know if where you end up is where you're supposed to be? If not, you and your future will end up a mess. Then all too often you will end up trying all kinds of other things, hoping to feel good about yourself for accomplishing *something*.

An Effective Ministry

Over the years, I have seen so many leaders do things because the "call" to do what they were supposed to do was not what they thought it should be. Therefore, they changed their course and diversified their efforts. Diversification is okay, but only if directed by God and not just because the results do not feel very good. So our feelings subvert the "call" and the "job," and we fail to do what God has for us to do. This not only keeps the real plan that God has for you from ever coming about but also often wastes most of your time. Oh sure, you are a minister, but not the very effective one you could have been.

Jesus said that a house divided against itself won't stand. This can be true about your ministry, and the principle applies to everything, including your effectiveness. Stop and think about this: do we just want a ministry, or do we really want an effective ministry?

"Effective"—what a word. It means the ability to produce results, and it says so much. Is not our God effective in everything? Of course He is, and He desires for us to be effective in His church. In the parable of the talents in Matthew 25:28, He gave the servant who made the most of what he had the talent of the one who had squandered his. Obviously, God wants us effective and successful.

Look at the Apostle Paul. As you already know, he had this great mandate from God to bring the revelation of grace to the church. How many times do you think Paul asked himself how he was going to get this done? He might have said to himself, "I'll travel to the known groups of believers and tell them," which he did. But we know there was not enough time in one man's lifetime to reach the world. Keep Paul's era in mind—there was no Internet, cell phones, social media, or even books, newspapers, TV, or radio. It was just his voice, one on one. Then, on top of that, God had him thrown into jail. What was God doing? What could He be saying? Could He be saying something to the generations that are to follow Paul about being effective?

> Effectiveness comes when we do God's plan and His will even when it is doesn't fit with our thinking or our desires for our future.

Effectiveness comes when we do God's plan and His will even when it is doesn't fit with our thinking or our

desires for our future. Remember, it is His view of **good and evil** that we need.

Let me review. I have defined *good* as "God's will done God's way." That would mean evil should be defined as "anything contrary or opposite to God's will or ways." I believe we could say that evil is any perversion of truth, and we know that Jesus defined truth in John 17:17 as God's Word. Satan has been perverting truth from the time of his fall.

> *Your heart was lifted up because of your beauty; You corrupted your wisdom for the sake of your splendor; I cast you to the ground, I laid you before kings, That they might gaze at you. You defiled your sanctuaries By the multitude of your iniquities, By the iniquity of your trading; Therefore I brought fire from your midst; It devoured you, And I turned you to ashes upon the earth In the sight of all who saw you.*
>
> Ezekiel 28:17-18

Here we see everything that God gave Lucifer was truth and very good, but Satan took the truth of God's goodness and perverted it. Because of his action, he became evil and corrupted himself.

The Call of Distraction

Effectiveness comes when we have clarity about our call and are faithful to respond to it. Do not let yourself get distracted from the plan and the will of the Lord. If you do, then you will find yourself working at things that will cause you to neglect what it is God desires you to do. And remember, anything contrary or opposite to God's will or ways is sin.

For example, I have known many pastors who have stopped pastoring for days and even months to write books that never went beyond their own churches. Perhaps this was not an effective effort because it became a supplement to what they were to put their attention on. I have watched many frustrated pastors leave their pulpits and travel to preach to other congregations, taking valuable time away from building their own church. Sometimes, the feeling of being accepted as a guest speaker may fulfill a need to feel good about ourselves. It can be difficult staying put in your own pulpit when there doesn't seem to be much fruit. I know ministering in other places isn't a wrong thing to do; it can be exactly what God would have for them. But here is my point: We must ask if it is the will of God for us to do it, or if it's just something that feels good. Remember "good"? God's will done God's way.

I wonder how Paul felt about himself as he sat in prison writing one little letter to one little group of people at a time. He truly had no idea that his writings would be read by millions of people every day for thousands of years. I believe that he is read by more people each day than all the other writers combined. Wow!

In order to be truly effective in God, sometimes we must set aside what we feel or what we think and wait for the right directions from God. That, my friends, is so hard, and that is where you must know that you are "called" to do what it is that God would have you to do.

I will say again: it is not bad to "preach out" or to write a book or develop a TV program for the Lord. If God called you to do it, *you'd better do it!* It becomes wrong when you're doing it to please people or to please yourself. Our job is to please *God*. Isn't it from Him that all things are fulfilled for Him and by Him (Col. 1:19-20)?

Keep in mind that when God calls you to do something, He will give you all you need to do it. He will give you all the approval and recognition that you will need to fulfill his plan.

I don't believe that God is looking for someone to build the Kingdom of God through human effort or fleshly ideas; that again would be a throwback to the knowledge of the tree of good and evil. Human enthusiasm and effort in the building of His kingdom amounts to no effort at all. What is pleasing to God is God-directed human effort and enthusiasm. Now *that* is effectiveness!

Here is a fun question: I wonder if Paul would have written so much if he had not been in jail? Maybe he would have filled his time up with other things, and he wouldn't have been able to write as he did. I think God knows what He is doing and is worthy of our trust as leaders.

For us, we must believe *"the steps of a righteous man are ordered of the Lord"* (Psalm 37:23).

Chapter 4

The Development of Your Heart

Being effective in Christ requires the development of the human heart. This development can take great time and, often, great pain—great time, because it can take a lifetime and great pain because it becomes an exercise in uprooting our personal comforts. It is much like doing those things that you know God would have you do even when you just don't feel like doing it. You know it is right, but that doesn't make it fun.

Before David had any idea that he had been chosen by God to be King over Israel, God was already speaking about him to King Saul through the Prophet Samuel: *"But now your kingdom shall not continue.* **The LORD has sought for Himself a man after His own heart,** *and the LORD has commanded him to be commander over His people, because you have not kept what the LORD commanded you"* (1 Samuel 13:14).

Wow, this is just a young man on the hills of Judea watching his father's sheep. He had no idea that the Great God of the Universe had selected grand things for him. I wonder what would have happened if David started to plan it all out for himself on how he would accomplish being the next king that followed King Saul?

By the way, King Saul is a perfect example of a person who tried to minister to God's people by his own thinking (remember "good"), and not a man who followed after God's own heart. He failed big time, and so will we if we don't get our directions from the Master Kingdom Builder.

After the great Samuel anoints young David to be king over Israel, David does not go out and try to fulfill his calling, he does not try to exalt himself in the eyes of the people, and he does not try making it happen by man's methods (like putting on Saul's armor for example in 1 Sam 17:38-39). He does something amazing—he goes back to the sheepfolds and even lays his life down for those dumb sheep! It was there that God started to develop the heart of this great followshipper. On the hills of Judea, this young boy began the development of a tender heart for God.

Following After God's Heart

Whom God chooses, He develops. He does this often in the most unusual ways, and there is always time for heart development. I'm not sure when it ever stops. For David, it was on those hills of Judea, just outside of Jerusalem.

I want to spend the rest of this chapter looking at David as a model of followship.

#1) **Seclusion.** The first thing that God used to develop David's heart was Seclusion. Stop and think about it—David was all alone, just him and God. God had him right where He wanted him, a place where God could be heard. Can you imagine a training ground where it is just you and God?

How about Paul in the wilderness with God for years, or Moses, or even Joseph? The development of the heart is so very important to the activity He wants from you.

Today, we have lost the art of listening. We are very seldom in a place of quiet where we can hear from God. Everything is loud, fast, and ever-changing. Under these circumstances, how can we ever expect to hear clearly from God?

> Today, we have lost the art of listening.

The other day I was in a busy restaurant with some friends for lunch. After I ordered, I sat back and noticed another pastor sitting by himself. I went over to say hello and invited him to join us. He declined and said that he needed this time to prepare for his upcoming message. I finished my greeting and went back to my table. As I sat there and ate, I kept on noticing how many interruptions he had: server, menus, food, noise, refills, and so much more. Maybe he could hear from God at that restaurant, but I know I could not. I would be too afraid to miss something that God had for me.

I think that hearing from God is more important often times than speaking to God. Is not hearing an important part of prayer? In my times of prayer, I had to learn to shut my mouth and shut myself away so I could hear from God.

Let me give you a personal example. When I felt the call of God to pastor, it was so simple that I never knew it was a call. God wanted to use me to help others get close to Him. Is that a call? In my mind, I thought a call should be something big, like reaching the whole world! Something that booms at you and shakes you to your very core. That's not what it was for me; it was just, "Help others get close to Me."

I didn't understand that helping others get close to God is where He wanted me to start. As I remained faithful to obey the simple things He told me to do, He began to build my future as a pastor.

In reality, if I had known what pastoring really was all about, I very likely would have run like Jonah and taken my chances! I was so ignorant and foolish that it would take a lot of work and time for God to develop any kind of heart in me.

One of the big problems I faced was not having any training or others to rely on, except for God and my wonderful, godly wife, Deby. That turned out to be a good experience, not a bad one.

#2) Boredom. The second thing that God used to develop David's heart was boredom. Can you imagine that a boring, dull, colorless place could teach you anything? Can you imagine how dull life must have been watching dumb sheep? Every day, the same routine, over and over again. Even after David was called and anointed by Samuel to be king, he ends up back with the sheep.

What would attract him back to the sheepfold time and time again? It couldn't have been excitement or fulfillment; I believe it had to have been the presence of God. No matter what the surroundings were, David had found the presence of God. Want proof? Think about all the inspired writings and eternal songs that came from those hills.

So what is the lesson here? In boredom, in dull places where seemingly nothing is happening, (much like the daily grind of pastoring), you can be in a great place to find His presence. Unlike Adam and

Eve who wanted "more," a young shepherd found the secret of fulfillment and satisfaction just in being in God's company.

What do you learn in a boring place? Often you're going to learn how to have confidence that God is making something happen on your behalf that you can't see.

In today's world, we hate boring times, and instead of finding God, we find something to entertain ourselves.

Paul writes, "*Now to Him who is able to do exceedingly abundantly above all that we ask or think, according to the power that works in us*" (Ephesians 3:20).

The writer of Hebrews says, "*But without faith it is impossible to please Him, for he who comes to God must believe that He is, and that He is a rewarder of those who* **diligently seek Him**" (Hebrews 11:6).

I use these verses to make a point. Note that the verse doesn't say "God is a rewarder of those that just work for him" but "seek" Him. Working is one thing, but there needs to be time to seek Him. I found that one of the best places to seek Him is in the "city of time and state of boredom."

This is possibly one of the most difficult things for pastors or any modern Christian to do. It sounds so simple, but is it? My wife Deby and I will have some time on our hands, and it won't be very long before one says to the other, "What do you want to do?" The answer is almost always the same: "I don't know, what do you want to do?" We go back and forth until someone makes a suggestion that fits, and off we go.

Americans like to stay busy. We are the only people in the world that have storage units for all of our junk and old hobbies that we don't do anymore. We work at finding things of interest to do every day. We just don't like to stop and take time for God. Yes, it *feels* boring. That is why God, who knows us intimately, initiated the Sabbath so mankind would have to rest and receive from Him.

Our culture dislikes being bored, and that is why we spend billions on every type of entertainment to keep us occupied. I believe that kind of attitude keeps us from true godly development in our hearts. We must push past that "Garden" feeling and do what is "good."

Boring is only boring if you haven't connected with God. If and when you connect, you are no longer bored but on the greatest adventure you will ever experience! That is why David returned to the sheepfolds over and over again. In his connection with God came the lesson of great trust and faith. No wonder he could face the lion, the bear, Goliath, and years of running from King Saul.

Keep in mind that David was forced into being a shepherd; it was his job in his family. But he didn't run from it; he ran *to* it. Why? Because that's where he met up with God. That is where all the songs came from—inspired songs because God talked to him and he was in a place to talk back to his God.

> I have found that in insignificance comes great dependency from the truly significant one—Jesus.

The lesson from dull places I learned from David and from pastoring is to remember that when I am bored, that might be a great opportunity to learn from God.

#3) Inattention. The third thing that God used to develop David's heart was inattention. In this place, you will find yourself where no one knows you, and, seemingly, no one cares. I heard a man describe it once as being a nobody that no one knows. It becomes a place of personal insignificance. I have found that in insignificance comes great dependency from the truly significant one—Jesus.

When the great prophet of God, Samuel, went to David's father, Jesse's house, Samuel asked Jesse and his sons to join him for the sacrifice. *"And he said, "Peaceably; I have come to sacrifice to the LORD. Sanctify yourselves, and come with me to the sacrifice."* **Then he consecrated Jesse and his sons, and invited them to the sacrifice"** 1 Samuel 16:5.

You know the story—Jesse brings seven of his sons but not the eighth. His own father didn't even see David as important!

I personally can't imagine that David's father didn't know David was a very spiritual person. In David's life, almost everything wrapped around God. Do you think when David was at home he somehow changed and didn't talk about God? I don't think so. Look at the battle with Goliath; you see that everything that comes out of his mouth is about God. So I believe his father knew that his son David had a special relationship with God.

Why wasn't David invited to the sacrifice to God? Maybe no one, not even in his own family, thought much of him. But God did, and God had already seen him, talked to him, and loved him.

I wonder how many pastors are out there, and they are nobodies that no one knows? The truth is, like David, God knows them and has a great plan for them. Sadly, so many give up because they don't fit the success picture that people carry in their minds. We can think we are not talented or gifted or smart, and our personalities don't fit the image that we have in our thinking. We say to ourselves, "Why try? I will just fail; I am not equipped for this." Often, we just give up. I believe that many can understand that kind of thinking. We might say something like, "If God wanted me to do it, then I would have been given the desire and the talent to accomplish it."

Shouldn't we be thinking that the talent and gifting, and even the drive and personality, all should come from God? But here is how it works—we just put in the "natural" and God puts in the "super," and now you have supernatural results. The truth is God doesn't want to do something by Himself; He wants to work with you. The Bible says we are co-laborers with Christ. Sometimes God will select the most unlikely person to carry out his plan—usually a person who is not what you would think. Like you and me or even David.

Generation after generation, we don't seem to change. We know the truth because we read it, but we always seem to go back to that Garden experience. We judge for ourselves what is good and what is evil. What we decide for ourselves the way it should or shouldn't be.

What if God is looking for a person whose only desire is to follow Him? Just simply follow Him. Stop and think for a moment—was that not exactly what He wanted in the Garden? And is that not exactly what he found in David, who became the greatest King Israel has ever known?

Paul writes,

> *Where is the wise? Where is the scribe? Where is the disputer of this age? Has not God made foolish the wisdom of this world? For since, in the wisdom of God, the world through wisdom did not know God, it pleased God through the foolishness of the message preached to save those who believe. For Jews request a sign, and Greeks seek after wisdom; but we preach Christ crucified, to the Jews a stumbling block and to the Greeks foolishness, but to those who are called, both*

Jews and Greeks, Christ the power of God and the wisdom of God. Because the foolishness of God is wiser than men, and the weakness of God is stronger than men.

For you see your calling, brethren, that not many wise according to the flesh, not many mighty, not many noble, are called. But God has chosen the foolish things of the world to put to shame the wise, and God has chosen the weak things of the world to put to shame the things which are mighty; and the base things of the world and the things which are despised God has chosen, and the things which are not, to bring to nothing the things that are, that no flesh should glory in His presence. But of Him you are in Christ Jesus, who became for us wisdom from God—and righteousness and sanctification and redemption—that, as it is written, "He who glories, let him glory in the LORD."

1 Corinthians 1:20-31

Let me show you how messed up I was so you can see how God can use a man who is just willing to follow Him.

When I was young, I thought for sure that I would make my living from playing professional baseball. I was a good player, above average, and I loved the game and worked hard to become a major league player. I didn't care about school or any kind of education. The truth is that I got through high school because the teachers of those days wanted to see me play baseball. I was an asset to the school team. When I graduated from high school, I had a fifth-grade reading level. That would be equivalent to a nine or ten-year-old's reading ability. "Forget college, who needs it? I'm going to be a great baseball player," I thought to myself.

After high school, I did sign a professional baseball contract, played three years in the minors, and washed out by the age of nineteen. Finished! And when you're out, boy, you are really out. No one cares about you; you are just gone. The baseball that I knew as a child was pure fun, but it changed, and the great game become a hard business filled with dog-eat-dog ambitions.

Life after that was not much better. I could get good jobs but had a hard time with marriage. Since I have already shared my testimony in the introduction, it's enough to say that I felt like I might be the world's biggest loser and certainly a nobody that nobody knew. I thought, after having messed up my life at such an early age, who could ever want me, and how could I ever have a life of any importance?

> Success is not about the ability you have, the talent you possess, your looks, or even the education of a believer; it is all in the following of the one true and great God, Jesus.

The only asset that I had was my growing love for the Lord. I felt that He still loved me, and throughout the day I could sense His peace, which kept me alive. Church had become a breath of fresh air in my life. Thank God for the pastors that paid the price to have church for people who are broken like me.

I said all of this to show how God can take the lowest of the low, a person that no one knew or even wanted to know. He made me to live and experience a great life that has touched the world, and I am so grateful and blessed to have been privileged to help build the kingdom of God.

If God could use a fool like me, how much more can he use you? You see, people may not know you, but *God* knows you. Success is not about the ability you have, the talent you possess, your looks, or even the education of a believer; it is all in the following of the one true and great God, Jesus.

In Mark 9:23 we read, *"If you can believe, all things are possible to him who believes."* How foolish it is for us to forget this simple truth and think for ourselves the way things should be or not be.

What does it take for us to truly follow God? The answer is one very powerful word, **humility**— one of the Bible's most misunderstood words. Humility should be defined as "**dependency.**" When we are humble, we are so dependent on Him that we can't exist without Him at every level. Your heart says, "Without God, you're just not going to make it."

It is not someone who *says*, "I'm dependent on God," when in fact they make their own way. Another thing that humility is not is being a low life—someone who plays the role of being lowly and hopes God is in it. Words are cheap and easy to say, but the life expressions will always follow the heart. It is easy for God to see at what level of dependency we are at.

Humility is visible in how we do life. It is what we do because we are grateful as we truly see God as our source of everything.

I remember a time when I was a younger minister, I was asked to speak at one of the world's largest and most famous Christian events. To be honest, I couldn't have been more honored. What a privilege! I was so excited, and I wanted to yell, "Yes!" After all, there would be about 30,000 people in attendance, and who wouldn't want to minister to that many people at one time? As the leader of this great event was talking to me on the phone, I opened my mouth and these words came out: "What would you like me to share? And how much time do I have to talk to God and see if this is what He would want me to do?" Why did I say that? Why didn't

I just say "yes" and leave it at that? I'm sure it would be good for all parties, I thought to myself. There was a silence on the other end of the phone then I heard, "I'll get back to you." I waited and I waited, but he never called me back.

A few years later, his secretary called in advance to make me aware that this great leader was going to call me and I was not to say "no." Sure enough, he called again. This time my answer was filled with confidence. This time I said, "What would you like me to share and how much time do I have to talk to God and to see if this is what he wants me to do?" Sadly, the phone conversation ended, and I was never asked again.

Let me give a clear understanding, I never said "no"; it was just perceived as if I did. This truly great man of God was doing exactly what God told him to do. His events have changed the way we do church throughout the world. But for me, I needed to know that God wanted me there and that God wanted to contribute something through me. When I know that, then I know that it won't be a man preaching his best sermon; it will be a man speaking the words of God, and His presence will be on them. It won't be just good; it will be GODLY GOOD. Remember the Garden? Now that is the kind of "good" we all should be looking for.

I believe true humility is found in the makeup of every great man and woman of God. There is no way you can follow God until you submit yourself to humility, and humility translates to **dependency**.

When this happens, you are now ready to start from the true beginning—I call it **back to the Garden for the real future.**

In review, inattention brings you to a place where you realize that you can't rely on anybody or anything but Him. It is in those obscure places that one becomes **dependent** and grateful.

4) Physical Reality. The fourth thing that God uses to develop David's heart is physical reality. The battles that a child of God will face are generated in the Spiritual realm, but the battle is, most of the time, acted out in the physical. David's young life shows his heart and his courage as well as his trust in God. His place of facing death became a place to develop great courage.

Paul writes,

> For though we walk in the flesh, we do not war according to the flesh. For the weapons of our warfare are not carnal but mighty in God for pulling down strongholds, casting down arguments and every high thing that exalts itself against the knowledge of God, bringing every thought into captivity to the obedience of Christ.
>
> 2 Corinthians 10:3-5

David had to do this or die. Remember, David tells King Saul about his battle with the lion and the bear.

> "Your servant has killed both lion and bear; and this uncircumcised Philistine will be like one of them, seeing he has defied the armies of the living God." Moreover David said, "The LORD, who delivered me from the paw of the lion and from the paw of the bear, He will deliver me from the hand of this Philistine." And Saul said to David, "Go, and the LORD be with you!"
>
> 1 Samuel 17:36-37

His father is very wealthy because not everybody could graze their sheep on the hills of Judea just a couple of miles from the city of

Jerusalem. All the people, including the great prophet Samuel, knew Jesse, David's father. You had to be someone of importance to be known by this great prophet of God.

How many sheep did David watch? No one knows, but my guess is that it was a lot because of the wealth of the father. Young lambs are always about, and when a lion or bear came into the flock and grabbed one, trying to rescue the lamb would mean risking your own life. If we think about what David did, it can seem crazy.

Risking your life for something noble or heroic may be worth it. But to put your life in harm's way for a lowly *lamb*—who would do such a thing? Who would put themselves in that place where their life is at stake over something that is not very important? My life, to me, would be worth more than *all* those little sheep. With that attitude, I probably would not have even gotten into that fight. I would have said something like, "Go ahead and enjoy your meal; my dad won't know, and even if he did I'm sure he would say to me, 'Good call, Son. I don't think you should risk your life for a dumb sheep. You're my son, and I love you a lot more.'" Any half-decent father would have that attitude.

> Courage is only good when God becomes the source of our courage.

However, David is different than most of us, and we can learn from him. Keep in mind that he spent day after day with God—so much that he received the revelation of God's Word.

Courage is only "good" when God becomes the source of our courage.

When you are strong in God, then you are strong toward the enemy. When you are not strong in God, it is probably because you are not where you should be with Him. You are not as close as you used to be, and the battle takes on a new front. Then you start to make excuses and try to justify why you don't fight. If you do fight, it will be in the flesh and not the spirit, and you can never win a spiritual battle in the flesh.

When David kept God bigger than his physical reality, he won the battle. When he did not, he made decisions based on his natural thinking, and he got himself and his men in a lot of unnecessary trouble.

With us, when God becomes bigger on the inside of us than the problems on the outside, there will be no question about the outcome of the battle. Problems only become big when you allow your God to become small.

Sometimes we fail to note that, when we pray, it often is not about getting a quick answer. The fact is, after we seriously pray, most of the time we don't see the answer to the prayer. The reason we feel better right after is because we made God big again through our prayers. We got off the problem and back onto God as the answer to the problem. Now our God just became bigger than the problem. Try to keep it that way.

Godly courage comes when your God is bigger than your problem. The source of your courage comes from the presence of your God.

"The call" really is to follow God in whatever it is that God has you to do. When the Lord called me to pastor, I had to learn to keep my focus on Him. When others were doing great things for the Lord, and my church was not doing anything, when I felt ineffective and unimportant, when life was boring and I felt like a failure...in God's reality, I wasn't. As it turned out, He was doing what He does best, and that was developing my heart.

Without the development of the heart, there is but a small effort toward fulfilling your call. God wants to do great and mighty things through you in your ministry, but like David, we have to be willing to let Him take us through His training fields. We have all heard the great saying, "God builds the minister before he builds the ministry." He does it in seclusion, boredom, inattention, and physical realities. It is never easy, but it is well worth it.

Chapter 5

The Order of Life

It's important for all followshippers to establish the right "order" for life and ministry. God's order is not always our order. Without godly order, everything in the future will fail, and your heart will break for the disappointment you feel.

God gets involved in His godly order, but you will soon find that He stays away from the activities that are out of His order. He just can't get involved.

It is similar to the foundation of the house. If it is good, then the rest of the house could have a chance to be good. If it is off, then the house has no chance of being right.

> It's important for all followshippers to establish the right "order" for life and ministry.

Everything in the Kingdom of God has order. If you take sand off the beach and put it in your eye, immediately you would know that something is wrong, and you would do all you can to correct it. If the problem is not corrected, the results become very bad, and eventually the eye will fail. In the Kingdom of God, it is the same. There are biblical principles here that we need to recognize.

In Galatians 6:7-9 Paul writes,

> *Do not be deceived, God is not mocked;* **for whatever a man sows, that he will also reap.** *For he who sows to his flesh will of the flesh reap corruption, but he who sows to the Spirit will of the Spirit reap everlasting life. And let us not grow weary while* **doing good,** *for in due season we shall reap if we do not lose heart.*

Look at "doing good" in verse nine. Remember, what is "good"? It is what God says, not what we think. This doesn't mean that you throw out your brain, but it does say that your thinking must line up with what God says. His will, want, and ways have become your will, want, and way. That is called "order."

So with that in mind, what you sow becomes very important. Your order to life may be different then God's order, and if that is the case then God can't and won't bless you. Why? Because if you're out of sync with God and He blessed you, then you would think you are okay with God, doing the right thing, and you would never change. You would just keep on doing what you are doing (which is wrong) over and over again. Because your priorities (order) are wrong, the outcome of your life will be different then what it could have been.

Being less than blessed is how most leaders live their lives. They don't say that, but deep down inside they know it. As I said, most pastors are living lives that consist of just staying alive. Trying to make ends meet becomes the goal. All the time, deep down inside they are asking where God is in this whole effort.

As pastors, we watch over the church, we preach the Word of God, we are passionate to the call with all that is in us, and we put up with some stupid and often rude sheep. We love God and truly want to serve God, and I'm sure we would give up or do anything we could to please Him. How could something be wrong, and why aren't we blessed? I hear this question many times in talking to pastors.

In Exodus chapter thirty-two we see the people worshiping the God who brought them out of Egypt—the right God, but the wrong way, and it almost cost them their lives. I think that we can build our ministries to the right God but do it the wrong way, and end up wasting our lives.

For many, we do big things in our hearts, but often it is the little things that trip us up. Little things that we don't even recognize can ruin the very thing we want most.

In the book of Canticles (we know this book as the Song of Solomon) we see the "bride," the Shulamite, talking to her brothers in the form of a request: "*Catch us the foxes, the little foxes that spoil the vines, for our vines have tender grapes*" (Song of Songs 2:15).

She says, "our vine has tender grapes." Another understanding might be they are young, not ready for the full picking. That's why I said that it is important to start right in the beginning. Get the order of your ministry (priorities) right. Because if you don't, the little foxes will ruin your effort.

Most of us don't understand that it is not the big foxes that cause the most trouble, because they are held back by the fence; it's the little ones who have a little nose that goes under the fence and can eat at the trunk of the vine until it falls over and the grapes lay on the ground where the other foxes can now reach them.

The real tragedy is not the loss of the grapes. That is a real shame, but the real loss is the entire grapevine. All the years of growth are now at a total loss, and that is exactly what the enemy wants for you. It is the little things that might take you out.

How easy it is to want to just go forward and not consider the foundation that we are going to build our ministry on. Order, once again, is not established by man but by God. Our thinking and our feelings, our wants and our desires must be set aside for God's will. That is not easy!

With all of that being said, let's get into the order of God, for all of our lives, especially pastors.

Order #1: Your God

"Of course," you say, "that's an easy one." We all know the scripture that says, *"And now, Israel, what does the LORD your God require of you, **but to fear the LORD your God, to walk in all His ways and to love Him, to serve the LORD your God with all your heart and with all your soul**"* Deuteronomy 10:12 .

So we see it is a complete commitment to Him. No questions asked or needed. Case closed.

But you also see the words *"serve the Lord your God."* So it's not only who you're committed to, but also what you do and how you do it. That is why the word "serve" is used. It is like the Lord is saying love and respect Me with all of your heart and soul. And from that position, your service begins.

And from here out is where a lot of pastors mess up, for it is not our love that is the issue but our "serve" that often become the problem. The "serve" starts with order and ends in order.

Order #2: Your Spouse

So many times, I have heard that the wife becomes the human sacrifice to the ministry. And here is where this gets a little sticky. I have actually heard men say to their wives that they need to be a sacrifice to the importance of the ministry. Some may not come out and say it as this pastor did, but they act it out. And you must understand that our human actions speak louder than our words.

Do not confuse the ministry by mixing it up with God. Ministry is what you do; God is whom you live for.

> Do not confuse the ministry by mixing it up with God. Ministry is what you do; God is whom you live for.

The union of a husband and a wife says so much. As you know, marriage in itself speaks of Christ and the Church, which will eternally speak of the goodness of God. The bride and the groom become important, as this is a witness to the world and the Church. Just think about this—the Church watches you both. They hunger for a righteous marriage example. That will become such an attraction to this lost and misled generation whose only example of marriage has been defined in America by a court of law, nine Supreme Court judges that were not even elected by the people. They have defined marriage to the people, never taking God, the creator of marriage, into their account.

Would it not make sense that if you want to define something you would go to the creator of that thing that you want to define? Scotch tape is defined by 3M Company, the Wright brothers defined flying, and someone like McDonalds defines a hamburger. Marriage cannot be defined by anyone but God.

As a pastor, I wanted to display my love for my wife—not just at home but also in front of the church. We will worship sometimes holding hands or just holding each other. The Bible makes it very clear that we are one, so I worked at making room for her in the ministry.

I always refer to her as "My Deby." She is me, and I'm her, and everyone knows it. And over the years it has protected the ministry and built it, for it shows a healthy relationship with God as our base (order).

On the other hand, you have seen the wives that have been trampled by the ministry. They end up hating the ministry and their children end up hating it also.

When there is a love for God and a love for your spouse, the ministry just works. The people become very happy and secure. The wife is happy and the children grow up strong in the ways of the Lord. What could be better?

Where there is a healthy marriage, there is a healthy ministry. When ministry is healthy, it just grows.

Order #3: Your Children

Remember, we are talking about godly order. How important is His order for your children? They are your next generation, and they will depend on two things: how they see your commitment to God and how they see your commitment to your spouse.

You are the family hero. No one else can or should take that place. All good fathers take care of their children; they should provide and protect their children. It says it all through the Bible. From the beginning to the end, God the Father shows us how He takes care of His family. And His actions speak louder than any words.

Like our spouses, we also never need to put our children on the offering block as sacrifices for our ministry. When we do that, the ministry is doomed to failure, and the children will grow to hate the ministry and maybe never have that personal relationship with Jesus—all because their lives were out of order.

We had to set boundaries in the lives of our children. These boundaries said what they could do and what they couldn't. Note what I said: their mom and their dad set the boundaries, *not* the children. It is amazing to me to see how many children set their own lifestyles. I heard a parent say that when the child gets older he can make up his own mind as to whether they accept God or not. That is so foolish! The enemy works on these children over time, and we when we do not set their order and boundaries, we do very little to be that example and that person they can trust to set the course for them. They are too young to make up their own minds. We always need to be godly parents.

The Bible says, *"as for me and my house, we will serve the Lord"* (Joshua 24:15). There is no debate about it. There is no choice about that in my home.

I always remember spending quality time with my children, not quantity. Quality is always better then quantity. Quality says I love you. I remember always trying to hold them, even when we were just watching TV. I refused to bring the ministry home with me or show the worry that I was carrying or the disappointment that comes with the ministry. Mama and I would talk about the problems, but not in front of the children. They only knew comfort and security. Our children had no idea what I was going through in order to provide for them.

My Deby and I worked at loving each other in front of our children and the church. Today, all our children are serving the Lord—their choice, by the way, and most of them are pastors. Healthy pastors at that! All of them are raising their own children. We have twelve grandchildren, (ten grandsons, two granddaughters) and one great-granddaughter. How cool is that?

God honors parents who raise their children in the ways of the Lord. He loves the generations; He is the God of Abraham, Isaac, and Jacob after all.

Keep the right order in your life, and God will bless the house—both houses, His and yours—and that is what you want. You know it, but you are going to have to work at it.

Order #4: Your Ministry or Your Job

Here is where most people make their mistake. Keep in mind the order so far—God, spouse, and children. The ministry is not God; it is your position or call or job. It is what God has asked you to do for the rest of your life. But it is not God Himself; it is the will of God for you while you are here on this planet.

> The ministry is not God; it is your position or call or job.

Your relationship with God should NOT be based on how well you do your job. It should be based on Him and how well He has done *His* Job. It is called "salvation." We sometimes forget this little truth. I remember a time when I was so caught up in the church that I was consumed by the wants that I had for the church. More growth had become my focus. Without growth, it was as if I was personally failing with God. But there was no growth in the church, and I was taking it personally. Everything was starting to fall apart.

My relationships with my wife, my children, even with God were starting to strain. Why? I thought I was doing and caring about what God wanted. Church growth—how could that be wrong? It isn't! What was wrong was my life's *order*. I had put the *ministry* in the place of *God*. The ministry had become my God, above my wife and my children. I was so out of order that everything started to fail and the church had stopped in all of the areas of true growth.

I remember the time and the place when I met up with God about it. It was on a walk on a dirt road up from my house after a church service on Sunday. He wasn't talking, but I was. I was complaining about everything, then finally got to the real issue, my life's priorities—and me. Surprisingly from the inside of me, something burst out at God. "I am not losing my wife or my children for this bunch of people who are here today and gone tomorrow. Forget it. I'm not going to give up my life for this ministry. If you want me to quit, well, I'll quit. My wife and my children are more important than this ministry. And that is the way it will be, God. And one more thing, You're not the ministry. You're my savior, my God, and my first love, period."

He didn't say a thing. He didn't have too; I was back on track. I knew something was up because I felt like I was free and back in order. Over the next two months, the church grew from 800 people to 2100 people. Wow, what a lesson for me to learn...but did I?

When churches grow, we pastors get so excited that we forget the order of God. I have had to start over many times with repentance and then work at getting back to God's proper order. I have found that is what God blesses.

Chapter 6

Learning How to Pastor

Learning how to pastor is a very deep subject usually not taught or learned in seminary or Bible school, yet learning on the job can be very difficult. Many don't last long enough to make it because there just isn't anyone around to help them. While I can't teach you in one chapter everything about how to pastor that it took me half a lifetime to learn, here are some good thoughts that I'm confident will cut down your learning time.

There is a big, but very important subject, to start with—a commitment to the office. Truthfully, the rest of this writing is about this big subject. I personally believe that 90% of your training will come on the job, and from now on I will try to discuss subjects that pastors have a tendency to overlook, causing their development and learning time to increase.

Sometime back, Deby and I were on a little vacation with my son Luke, his wife Stacy, and their two little children. We were in the eastern High Sierra's traveling to an old ghost town. While on a winding road, we spotted a sheep that stuck in a mud hole in the middle of this vast and obscure mountain valley. The flock had moved on and left that sheep behind to fend for himself. As we drove by, we all felt sorry but thought it would get out on its own and join the flock.

After a few hours of walking through the old town, we went back to the car and headed out. When passing that very spot, we all saw that the sheep was still there and very stuck. We all wanted to see him free and joined back up with his flock. But he hadn't. We all spotted him, still there and struggling to free himself. As we drove by, everyone shouted for me to stop the car!

I stopped but tried to explain that there wasn't anything that we could do because of the terrain and the fences. Before I could even get the words out of my mouth, they were all out of the car leaving me behind with my two small grandchildren. All three, Deby, Luke, and Stacy, were running down this embankment, crossing the pasture, and jumping the water run-off streams. I have no idea how they got over the fence. But they did.

They were quickly there alongside that big old sheep, trying to get him out. As I parked the car at the top of the embankment, I watched as they tried over and over again to free him. With each try, they got dirtier—covered with mud from the stream he had gotten himself stuck in. The mud was now on them, and the stream of water that flowed by had soaked them.

Finally, after a long time, they got a tree limb under him and lifted him out. This muddy, wet, and cold sheep didn't move for a little while. Stunned and over-exhausted, he ran away from the strangers that just saved his life, for surely the wolves of the Sierras would have eaten him that night.

As the team made their way back to the car, they were dirty, cold, wet, and covered with mud—but very fulfilled with what they had just done. They saved the life of Mr. Stuck Sheep.

Over the years, I've thought many times about that rescue. The three of them did the work, but God spoke volumes to me about the care of His sheep. Here is some of what He said.

Sheep Are Helpless

First, I had to see that these sheep are helpless; they have no defensive weapons or even offensive weapons. They seem to have no protection at all. They have no claws or sharp teeth. They have no armor as some animals have. They have no real horns or strong legs for kicking. They are just fluffy little things ready for wolves to eat them. In the case of Mr. Stuck Sheep, it would appear that the only defense this guy had was being in the flock with a good shepherd watching out for him.

The closer the shepherd is to the sheep, the safer the sheep are. That why in Psalms 23:4 says, *"Yea, though I walk through the valley of the shadow of death, I will fear no evil; **For You are with me; Your rod and Your staff, they comfort me.**"*

The sheep are comforted because the shepherd is with them. The rod and staff of the shepherd are at work. It not only keeps them on the right path but also fends off any unwanted evil.

In the case of Mr. Stuck Sheep, his shepherds were not close by; they had moved on and didn't care about him and left him for the evil that was to be upon him. So, the closer the shepherd is to the sheep, the safer the sheep should be.

Sheep Need a Shepherd

I also noticed that sheep love to wander off by themselves and bring tragedy to themselves. For sure they will get stuck somewhere, in some mud hole or in some rocks, and even eat and drink the wrong things. That's why Psalms 23:2-3 says, *"He makes me to lie down in green pastures; He leads me beside the still waters. He restores my soul; He leads me in the paths of righteousness For His name's sake."*

How important is the "Good" Shepherd? The sheep's entire direction, safety, and complete restoration of the thinking come from Him. That is why it is so important for us under-shepherds to practice followship.

Taking this position lightly would be tragic for the sheep. That's why the "tree of the knowledge of good and evil" will only lead them to death. It's just what God said—not just spiritual death, from separation from God, but also early physical death, by making wrong decisions and getting wrong directions.

During the rescue of "Mr. Stuck Sheep," I went to find the shepherds only to find that they were in their trailer, drunk, and didn't even care about that sheep until I offered them some money to come and get him back to the flock. They were bad shepherds because the condition of the sheep was not important to them, only the money they could make. Money had become their motivation.

It is a funny thing that God is extremely interested in helpless and dumb sheep. He looks for those "good" shepherds who will care more about the sheep than themselves.

That is the very thing that makes David the greatest King Israel has ever known. He was a man who cared about what God cared most for, or as God said, "a man after my own heart."

There Are Different Kinds of Shepherds

Shepherds—how interesting they are! Could God have been saying something when he told two groups of people about the birth of His Son?

First, the three kings from the East. They were gentiles from a different land, bringing gifts of appreciation to this newly born King. Wow! That says to me that the world needs to see and appreciate this very special gift—Jesus!

The second group of people that He speaks to are shepherds in the field. Picture this: a smelly, dirty bunch of men—rough, rugged, and weather beaten—who are willing to live with the flock.

God could have spoken to anybody, like the guards or the Levites or the priests. He chose to speak to the working shepherds. Could He be showing how important the Son is and how important the shepherds are who will take care of the sheep that the Son came for? I think so.

You Are in Shepherd Training

Learning to pastor is a lifelong education where you are a student, and Jesus, by His Spirit, is the teacher. How He teaches is through life's experiences that sometimes are not very pleasant and, of course, from His Word.

It is a life that must be about others more than about ourselves. Pastoring is about being there for God's people, not the people being there for ourselves. There are just not many people that want to or are even able to live that kind of life.

With education comes tests or times of examination; they show what you have learned and what is really in your heart. **A life lived is simply the words from your heart.** What you do speaks so much.

Until you pass the tests, you are unable to advance to the next level. When you pass the test, it is the proof that you are ready to advance. Everything will be tested or tried during the course of this adventure of pastoring.

School is only about education, but the "school of pastoring" is about your life—your heart and your thinking, as well as, what is important and is not important to you. You will learn how to deal with your issues—even the issues you didn't know you had! It is just the way of the Lord and the examinations that go along with the office of the pastor.

From this point on, we will discuss some of the lessons that a pastor must learn in order to fulfill his God-given goal.

Chapter 7

Every Pastor's Cause

So many things come at you. Most of these things will try to move you from what God has for you to do. If they can get you on a different path, you will never finish your race. Protecting your heart for your calling is as important as anything else you will do.

Every distraction cost lives (souls) and time. We all know the enemy is out to stop you, and if not stop you, then distract you so that you never accomplish your assignment. Staying focused on your assignment is critical to your accomplishment.

Distractions will cause you **to lose focus** on the clear directions that God has set out for you to accomplish. At the very least, they will slow you down and cause you to be frustrated and feel lost.

These distractions can even get and keep you out of order. (Remember: God, spouse, children, job/pastoring.) Moses had this problem with all the people, so he needed to get help so he could stay focused. Also, you may remember, so did the apostles when they were serving tables.

Let me give you some examples.

Commitment

> The depth of
> your commitment
> will define
> the importance
> of your call.

The depth of your commitment will define the importance of your call. (You should read that again).

Whatever God has called you to do, it will never get accomplished without a commitment to it. Commitment goes way beyond a desire or a want. A commitment is an action that one takes to see the results that God placed in your heart. It is God's plan, with your commitment behind it, which brings godly "good" results.

A lot of people have a different understanding of the meaning of commitment. The only meaning that puts us all on the same page is God's understanding of that word: Commitment is to undertake a "cause" with a dedicated whole heart.

In 1 Samuel 17:29, David is speaking to his brothers that are out to make fun of him and to cause him to doubt and question who he is and his God: "And David said, 'What have I done now? *Is there not a cause?'*"

The same cry comes out from the throne of God today: "Is there not a cause!" Of course there is and will be! For as long as there is a church on the face of the earth, there will be a cause and a need for men and women to respond to that cause.

The response is not to just say yes, but a yes must be a yes in the face of *everything* that says no, even the subtleties of distractions.

What does it mean to commit to the fulfillment of the cause of Christ?

Maturity

There is an enemy that wants to take the church captive, control the outcome of people's lives, and defeat the activity of the church so that it becomes impotent in all areas. He wants to reduce it at every turn of the road until it becomes so small that it only fits in a coffin.

This is what the future shepherd of Israel, David, learns in his first encounter with the enemy, Goliath. This enemy will defy the armies of the living God, trying to get them to become their servants, when they are to become only servants of the Most High God. The battle continues today, in a different form each time from the first battle (the Garden) to the last, in you and me and everyone in between, but with the same desired outcome.

The "office" that you work in has clear direction from the "Commander In Chief". It is to get God's people strong and to keep them strong. That is called **maturity.**

Ephesians 4:11-15 says,

> *And He Himself gave some to be apostles, some prophets, some evangelists, **and some pastors** and teachers, **for the equipping of the saints for the work of ministry,** for the edifying the body of Christ, till we **all come to the unity of the faith and of the knowledge of the Son of God, to a perfect man, to the measure of the stature of the fullness of Christ;** that we should no longer be children, tossed to and fro and carried about with every wind of doctrine, by the trickery of men, in the cunning craftiness of deceitful plotting, but, speaking the truth in love, **may grow up in all things into Him who is the head—Christ.***

Looking at this, you clearly see the "cause" and "plan" for us to follow. Protecting this cause and plan is tied to your commitment.

Every pastor's cause is to build God's people to maturity. Without maturity in God's people, there is little effort towards accomplishing His plan. So, how do we accomplish His cause? To build God's people to the place of "maturity"?

Let's start by defining maturity. Maturity is when the people of God understand and react accordingly by doing what God says to whatever they face. They do not do what our society says we should act like or what we have been taught by our parents or maybe what our education says we should be like. Mature people of God react accordingly by doing what God says, period! (Remember the tree in the Garden.)

But let's not use our definitions, because we all have different ideas, so let's let God define it for us.

Hebrews 5:12-14 says,

> For though by this time you ought to be teachers, you need someone to teach you again the first principles of the oracles of God; and you have come to need milk and not solid food. For everyone who partakes only of milk is **unskilled in the word of righteousness**, for he is a babe. But solid food belongs to those who are **of full age**, that is, those who **by reason** of use have their **senses exercised to discern both good and evil.**

Let me take a moment to explain so that we may be on the same page. In the first battle of David's life, (outside the bear and the lion) we see Israel's soldiers. They have no spiritual idea that they are in a battle for their lives, and it is *spiritual* one.

Note what they say in comparison to what David says. 1 Samuel 17:24 says, *"And all the men of Israel, when they **saw the man** [Goliath], fled from him and were dreadfully afraid."*

The failure of these men is not in the size of Goliath; after all, Goliath is what he is. It wasn't because they fled from him, and it wasn't because they were "dreadfully afraid"—this is just the human response to the true failure that had already set in. The failure came when they "saw the man." They saw something completely different than what David saw.

Now, read David's perspective in 1 Samuel 17:26: *"Then David spoke to the men who stood by him, saying, "What shall be done for the man who kills this Philistine and takes away the reproach from Israel? **For who is this uncircumcised Philistine, that he should defy the armies of the living God?**"*

David saw a man that had no God (uncircumcised), in contrast to the men of the army of Israel who had the undefeatable God with them. Also, note that he saw that armies of Israel not as an army of the territory, but completely differently—*"the armies of the living God."* David understood that he had a God on his side who is alive and active, not some dead god of fools. So what is there to be afraid of? That is how David saw the problem.

I have found that many people, including church leaders, see the natural more than the spiritual. But, remember what maturity is—it's being those *"who by reason of practice have their senses exercised to discern both good and evil."* Also remember that in their maturity they skillfully apply the Word of Righteousness to the situation. This equals MATURITY.

Maturity becomes impossible if people continue to approach it through the natural, for the victory we desire will never be accomplished by the natural. Or let me say it like this—the natural will never overcome in the spiritual. We were not made that way, and it just won't work that way. The natural can only be overcome by the spiritual. If anyone wants to change the natural and the obvious battle you see, it all starts with what are you focused on: the natural, which is so real, or the spiritual, which seems so crazy. (You already know that, it's just good to have someone remind you.)

Live Up to Your Calling

> Protecting the office will always start by acknowledging what you must accomplish and the life you must live to fulfill it.

Protecting the office will always start by acknowledging what you must accomplish and the life you must live to fulfill it.

Get ready. People will laugh at you, relatives will make fun of you, and the people that you thought were friends will show themselves not to be. By the way, the people who think they have the ministry of criticism and judgment will come out of the woodwork, but there is no ministry of criticism and judgment found in the Bible (Romans 14:4). This will all happen because you appeared to be strange and too spiritual, and that makes the natural in people very uncomfortable.

This exactly what happened to David. In 1 Samuel 17:28 we read,

> Now Eliab his oldest brother heard when he spoke to the men; *and Eliab's anger was aroused against David,* and he said, "Why did you come down here? And with whom have you left those few sheep in the wilderness? I know your

*pride and the insolence of your heart, for you have come down to **see the battle.***"

It's true he wanted to "see the battle," and he did, but he just saw it differently than his brothers or the men standing around listening to Goliath's taunts.

That very moment when you see things spiritually, you have taken the first step toward victory. Of course, the battle will still exist in the natural, but it will change in time. The battle becomes subject to change in God's timing. This becomes a battle against time that you will learn to fight.

All throughout Jesus's ministry you see that the spiritual overcomes the natural, not the natural overcoming Jesus.

What would life be like if we just saw the answer spiritually before we took action physically? David took action physically (naturally) after he won the battle spiritually. That's maturity. And that is the goal to attain in our churches. Remember from Hebrew 5:14 that we need to exercise our senses to see what is "good" and what isn't—or what is God and what is not God.

This is exactly where Adam and Eve failed—and took the rest of mankind down with them. And this is exactly the role of the church—to get God's people back to the directions from God.

Teach the Word to the Sheep

We are to bring the church to maturity—sounds so easy, doesn't it? But keep in mind that we are all sheep who love to wander or just get lost or try new clumps of grass over that hill or even get stuck in the mud. We are all like Mr. Stuck Sheep.

I'm sure you have heard this more than once: "Pastor, that was the best message and the best church service I've ever been in. See you for sure next week." And you never see them again.

Sheep! Sometimes they are a mess, and we have the job of trying to get into them the only thing that can straighten them out—God's Word. Thankfully, there are a lot of sheep out there. Talk about job security!

Funny, sometimes we try everything *but* His Word. Some might think they will mature if we become their friend or if we can find them a friend or maybe if we just preach harder or louder or give them a good church experience like fun or laughter or shorter church services or if they see us as successful or we put them in a spot to serve. Those are all good to help keep them around for a while so you can, while you have them, get the Word into them! That's the only thing that will make them mature to help them become more committed to church, for doing the work of the ministry (Eph. 4:12).

My father cut my hair for most of my young life. My dad was my barber. He was a very special man to me. When I sat in the chair while he cut my hair, he would tell me not to move around or he might cut my ear off or something. I was always a wiggle worm, and he would bop me on the head with his scissors and say, "Sit still." It never hurt me; it just kept me focused on not moving around so that I didn't get hurt.

Sometimes I feel like I would enjoy giving some people that "bop" on the head to keep them from moving around! Maybe that would help them to sit still so they can learn what God expects from them. Unfortunately, Deby won't let me!

Maturity is not easily attained. Like everything in the Kingdom that will produce godly results, people will resist it—and so will the enemy. And when I say resist it, I mean *resist it*! Sometimes we forget that the enemy doesn't want you or me to succeed. We can expect great resistance from everywhere.

So why doesn't God help us to fulfill His plan?

He does, but He doesn't do it with the flesh or in the natural. When it is all said and done, you, with Him, will win—but it will not usually be the way you thought.

So protecting the office and the anointing is vital to the task of bringing God's people to maturity.

> So protecting the office and the anointing is vital to the task of bringing God's people to maturity.

Chapter 8

The Calamity of Compromise

Compromise is an area that affects so many church leaders, and they don't even see that they are doing it. Things that get us to compromise will also keep us out of the anointing and His presence. And it will stop all church growth.

> Things that get us to compromise will also keep us out of the anointing and His presence.

Usually, it happens because of something that is not working as you might think it should, or maybe what you were expecting didn't happen in the time or place that you thought it should.

I find it fascinating how we have it all planned out for God. After all, "We got this," and all He has to do is get involved and do it, right? Wrong! Where do we get this kind of thinking? Could it be a "garden thing"? You know, we become "like God." As you know, He has it all planned out, and we just need to get in there and do it.

Remember what the serpent said in Genesis 3:5: *"For God knows that in the day you eat of it your eyes will be opened, **and you will be like God, knowing good and evil.**"*

Of course, that was a lie. When we respond in the flesh, we are not like the God that created the heavens and the Earth, but we keep trying. We design our everything and then want Him to get involved in it—almost as if He is to follow us, when, in fact, we are to follow Him. Remember "followship"? So when things don't come about as we think, we often start down the road of compromise.

In this case, the compromise that I'm talking about is accepting standards that are lower than God's. This brings us to a weakened and foolish state where we become less effective than we could have been.

Compromise is one of the church leader's biggest problems. We water down our commitment just to settle an issue we don't see coming to pass.

The Cave of Compromise?

Let's use David again as an example. This great man of God did compromise many times in his life, but he had other times, especially early in his life, when he stayed strong and committed to God's way and didn't listen to the other people who were trying to influence him.

In 1 Samuel 24, we find King Saul in hot pursuit of David again. For years now he has been running for his life and now has about 600 rag-tag men following him. These men are men that King Saul has been after for back taxes and unpaid bills; these men have lost everything. If they could just get rid of King Saul, they could go back to their farms and homes and villages, and their own beds. But now they, like David, are on the run for their lives.

King Saul has 3,000 highly-trained men with him. In the course of this pursuit, King Saul needs to relieve himself, so he goes into a cave where David and his men "happen" to be hiding out. They see King Saul, but King Saul doesn't see them. I can only imagine what they might have felt or thought. Maybe something like, "Standing in front of us is the answer to our prayers. With King Saul dead, we are free—free to go home back to our villages and farms and families. We can go back to our beds and not sleep on hard rocks anymore. Isn't this just what had been prophesied to David? This is a no-brainer; kill him and let us go home, out of this cold cave to our warm homes."

We read, "*Then the men of David said to him, "This is the day of which the LORD said to you, 'Behold, I will deliver your enemy into your hand, **that you may do to him as it seems good to you.'** "And David arose and secretly cut off a corner of Saul's robe*" (1 Samuel 24:4).

Isn't it just like God to leave it up to us as to what we will do? Our good or His "Good"—it was David's call. Then it says, "So David restrained his servants with these words, and did not allow them to rise against Saul. And Saul got up from the cave and went on his way" (1 Samuel 24:7).

What a choice David had to make! To rise up and please his men or to stay the course and please God.

Compromise is just justifying change to a commitment—but a commitment that has been watered down is no more than justified failure. My friend, there is only one road to follow, and no one said it would be easy.

During times of discouragement, watch out for the trap of compromise.

Compromise may seem right for a moment, but if you give time to your commitment and time to your thinking, you will know the way you should go. Don't let the feeling of overwhelming passion be the answer to His still small voice.

After Deby and I had pastored our first church for about five years, I turned that church over to our assistant pastor. Not knowing where to go and not having any money to get there, I really compromised my life. I told my wonderful wife that I was finished pastoring; it was a position with just too many disappointments and hurts. I told her that I felt that God was leading us to a new ministry, a television ministry that didn't deal with people directly. I explained that I didn't feel that God wanted me in front of the camera but behind it, and we should use what little money we had left to try to find a television station. She asked how we were going to obtain this station, and I told her we just had to find one first and then we'd figure out the rest. Being a great godly wife, she was just going to follow her compromised pastor husband. For the next three months of our lives, we chased after every kind of television station we could find.

After spending all of our money and having no success, I decided to go back to a real Christian television company and see how it all works. We saw that the Christian Broadcasting Network had a missionary conference going on and that we could attend and learn something about missions. We did, and I was very impressed and thought that maybe God wanted to send us to the mission field. But while I was there I thought I should try to see someone about a job.

I made an appointment with a vice president. While I was explaining my situation, he stopped me and said, "You're running from your call. You don't need a job; you have one—you're a pastor." No, I thought, I am finished with that—anything has to be better than that! But maybe I'll see if I am called to be a missionary.

After getting home, I got a round-trip ticket to Lagos, Nigeria, in Africa. I only knew one person there, another pastor who had a wonderful church in Lagos. I was there for two weeks, preached every day, and hated every minute. Missionary work was not for me. While I was on the west coast of Ghana, Africa, God spoke to me and said, "I want you to stop wasting time and go home. Become the pastor I want you to be—a pastor in America."

Those were the best words I ever heard—not so much about pastoring but about going home! I was so compromised; I had been hurt pastoring, and I just didn't want to get hurt again. I still didn't want to pastor, but I decided to do it until the church failed. It never failed.

Compromise is the Kryptonite to Your Future

We all know that we should not compromise, but many don't even realize we are doing it. So let me give you some ideas on how not to compromise and how to recognize it as slides into your life using the Bible as examples.

Compromise is a result of a weakening of the flesh, which comes by allowing your mind to meditate on things you should not be thinking. A great example is found in James 1:13-15 when he writes,

> Let no one say when he is tempted, "I am tempted by God"; for God cannot be tempted by evil, nor does He Himself tempt anyone. But each one is tempted **when he is drawn away by his own desires and enticed.** Then, when

desire has conceived, it gives birth to sin; and sin, when it is full-grown, brings forth death.

Note verse fourteen says *"drawn away"* through his thoughts. I believe this is when we are drawn away by ourselves. Verse fifteen tells us that a desire can become pregnant through thought and give birth to sin. Here is my translation of James 1, "Lust **entertained** breeds sin, and sin breeds death."

Let us take a look at the life of Joseph. Joseph was a young man alone in a strange country but blessed by God with great favor with God and man. His master, Potiphar, trusted him with everything, and when his wife comes on to Joseph, he easily turns her away. Note his words in Genesis 39:9: *"There is no one greater in this house than I, nor has he kept back anything from me but you, because you are his wife. **How then can I do this great wickedness, and sin against God**?"*

Where did this answer come from? Joseph was simply prepared mentally to combat anything contrary to his position. This doesn't just "happen"—he, like any red blooded man, saw her in the house many times, and he knew beforehand how to handle what was coming. Often times, we get a warning from God, but we treat it as if it's a game we can play with. Remember, when we entertain lust, we breed sin, and sin breeds death.

Compromise most easily enters the life of those who are unprepared. So be prepared! In 2 Corinthians 10:5, Paul says, *"**casting down arguments and every high thing that exalts itself against the knowledge of God,** bringing **every thought** into captivity to the obedience of Christ."*

Another example might be Abraham; God speaks to him about having a child. But in Genesis 17:18-19 it says,

And Abraham said to God, "Oh, that Ishmael might live before You!"

Then God said: "No, Sarah your wife shall bear you a son, and you shall call his name Isaac; I will establish My covenant with him for an everlasting covenant, and with his descendants after him.

Sounds like compromise to me! Abraham was saying, "I *have* a son; Ishmael is his name." But God says no way!

Here is my point: sometimes we **compromise when the natural seems easier then the spiritual.** But what could be more natural (easier) than God getting involved? Remember—back to the Garden thinking. Always see the spiritual as the *easier* way.

> We compromise when the natural seem easier then the spiritual.

One more quick point. **We compromise when we feel that God is not with us and we are on our own.** Remember when all the territories of Israel were compromised when their enemies wanted to "put out" their right eye (1 Samuel 11). They were going to let that happen because they felt alone, with no leader and no God. Living your life without your right eye says so much about a life that has been compromised. That's what the devil wants to do to your life. Stay strong, be of "good" courage, and watch what you are allowing in your thinking.

Chapter 9:

The World of Wrong Thinking

I've heard it said many times, and so have you, that the mind is the battleground for most fights. I don't know if that is true, but over the years of spiritual guidance (counseling), I'm sure that this takes up a large part of all battles.

To me, wrong thinking is when we think that we need something in our life other than God's presence in order to accomplish the task that is set before us. Sometimes we say things like we just need more money, or we need someone to give that big check, or if we just had more people all of our problems could be solved, and so on. You get the drift. We think about all the things that we think we need to have that bigger and better church. These kind of thoughts are not wrong; they are just out of order.

> When a thought takes the place of the real Answer, you must dismiss the thought until you get back to the true answer, Jesus.

When a thought takes the place of the real Answer, you must dismiss the thought until you get back to the true answer, Jesus.

We start to go down this road of wrong thinking when we make it personal, such as, "I'm not smart enough," or sometimes we say, "I don't have the right college degree," "I have no talent," or "I'm not as gifted as others are." We start to beat ourselves up, and the battle is already lost. When small thinking, evil thinking, or bad thinking becomes part of our makeup, we lose all battles. I'm sure most battles are lost before we really get into them.

Isn't that what was wrong with the Children of Israel when they came out of captivity? They still had a slave's wrong thinking—small mindedness. Even though they saw the hand of God in the miracles that He did for them, they could not get away from their wrong thinking.

When we naturally or carnally evaluate the problem and think the only way to solve the problem is natural or carnal thinking, we fail. As Christians, we are to find that better solution. If we don't, then the future is failure.

I think about the Children of Israel, and I see us today doing the same thing. The problem is clearly defined: no food, no water. Don't you think that God had the ability to sustain them in the wilderness without food and water? Most of us might say, I think so, or I guess so, because we do not clearly see the answer to that question.

But have you ever thought about Moses? He was on the mountain with God for forty days and nights, without food or water. Even the children of Israel thought he was dead. We all know that you can't live that long without water. But he shows up, after forty days, in really good shape. What could it have been that could keep him alive and looking great for forty days?

Here is what I believe—it was God's presence that kept him alive. I know, it doesn't fit with our thinking. Where did we get our own thoughts about how life works? I believe it comes from "The Garden"—from the tree of knowledge of good and evil or (New Testament) when we fail to have our senses exercised to discern what is "good" and what is evil.

I also believe that the answer for all things, including all problems, is found in His presence. His presence that brings on His anointing, and it is this anointing that becomes the future of the church. This truth always has been and always will be that "His presence sustains life." Believing God for your very existence is one thing, and I could do it, but then I get hungry and the battle changes. Maybe that is why the lost art of fasting is so real in our churches.

When you and I face problems in our church with the true answer in mind, "His presence will sustain this church," then the victory is just around the corner.

> When you and I face problems in our church with the true answer in mind, "His presence will sustain this church," then the victory is just around the corner.

The Anointing

When you protect the anointing, you are really protecting His presence.

At the time of this writing, Deby and I have lived in the San Bernardino, California, area for about forty years. Before we moved here, we lived in Santa Barbara, California. This is where we were married. The difference between San Bernardino and Santa Barbara is night and day. One is truly one of the best and most beautiful cities in America; the other is one of the worst cities to live in. The difference between the two is so great that I could go on for the next ten pages and still not cover all the difference. But here we are, and I wouldn't want to be anywhere else.

I always said if Jesus walked the streets of Southern California, He would walk in San Bernardino. It is a city that is broken in every area—dead if you will—and the only thing that can bring it back to life is Jesus.

Someone once asked me what I did so wrong that God would send us from Santa Barbara to San Bernardino. Well, maybe Deby and I are just crazy enough to see Him as all we will ever need. There was no anointing for us in Santa Barbara, but God showed up big time for us in San Bernardino. The anointing—His presence—is all you will ever need.

We did not think that way at first, of course. We, like everyone else, had our want list—you know, the things that we "needed" in order to be successful. We wanted to have people, money, fortune, fame, recognition, acceptance, and the approval of man.

For our church, we wanted a great music ministry and children's church and so on. These are not bad; in fact, these are the right things for a pastor to want. The error comes in how we try to get it. Again, the right thing the wrong way always equals failure.

Deby and I were once invited to minister at a friend's church outside of Houston, Texas. We were young, and to be honest with you, we didn't know what we were doing in our own church, let alone someone else's.

It was a conference, and we were featured as the guest speakers, which was a great honor. I'll never forget this one evening of ministry. Another guest speaker was to minister first, and then me. While I was listening to his message, he kept on saying that the church needed money or it couldn't exist—he was speaking of the church in general. Every time he said it, it rubbed me the wrong way. I should have just let it go, because I was a guest, and I should have just gone with the flow. After all, I'm not the Holy Spirit. But being young and very stupid, when it came my time to speak, I stood up and said, "What that man just said was a lie. The church doesn't need money it needs God!" Wow! How could I be so right...yet so wrong?

The passion and dependency for His presence that created my very existence has been developing in me from that day to now. By the way, those great and most kind hosts never invited me back, and I don't blame them.

God Fixes Bad Thinking

So there we were in this truly broken city with lots of broken people trying to figure out how to do life and how to build a church.

We didn't have a clue. We bounced around for years between the natural and the spiritual. It would seem that while I was in the pulpit teaching, I was spiritual...and then Monday came and we counted the offering. At first, I completely fell apart. I, of course, forgot the very truth I ministered just the day before. So when Monday came, I would be complaining to God about the lack of finances and asking questions like "How am I going to feed my children and put tennis shoes on their feet?"

Worse yet, for some crazy reason, I was asked to be on the board of another church in another town. After a board meeting, sometimes I just wanted to cry. They often had millions of dollars in the bank. We had nothing, living from week to week. Was I jealous? Yes! And at the same time, I was frustrated to the point of tears. I was truly happy for them but felt that I must be doing something wrong. What could it be?

I tell you, it was just *bad thinking* on my part. I felt that I needed big money to do big things, when in truth all I ever needed was my big God, who keeps everything alive by His presence!

After these board meetings, I wasn't so happy with God and like the children of Israel I complained and would, in anger, cry out, "It's not fair! I need food to exist!" In my case, it was money and people.

> God taught me to rest and to be at peace, for everything you could ever need or want is found in Him.

Now that I look back, I had no idea that God was teaching me something—something so great that it in itself would become the most important thing I could ever learn. It was more important than all the money in the world and more important than being the largest church in the world.

God taught me to rest and to be at peace, for everything you could ever need or want is found in Him. But here is how that works: **We find God first; we find the natural second.**

No More Cares

The Children of Israel saw everything from a natural perspective, and it kept them out of the place where God wanted to take them, the Promised Land. Because we more often than not do the same thing, we get their same results—no Promised Land.

God tells us, "*casting all your care upon Him, for He cares for you*" (1 Peter 5:7). He says that because we have a tendency to hold on to the cares. After all, how can the situation get resolved if I don't care about it, right?

Here is how this works—**if you carry the cares, then He can't.** He won't. He will not take from you what you want or what you need. He will let you just live with it. But we must realize that God **gives** to us what we want and what we need. We do not need to carry it; He will give it.

The other day, I was watching one of my grandchildren cry over a toy that he had dropped that he thought he needed. His mom got up and gave It to him and turned and said, "No big deal." My point is this—God will give us what we think we need because all things are "no big deal" to Him, so we end up carrying stuff we really don't want to carry.

So then He will let you carry the care. After all, you want it and feel you need to carry the care. He loves you, so He will just let you have it.

But what if it is not just your care, but His, and not your need, but His?

When that care becomes His, *He* will take care of it. How long do we have to wait for the tree of knowledge of good and evil to be recognized for what it is? And how long must we wait to go back to total dependency on Him?

The world of "wrong thinking" starts when we think He can't and He won't and that we need something besides His presence. The world of right thinking says His presence is all I need, and He will do what He wants when He wants. Right thinking is accompanied by the position of rest. Rest is the proof of your faith, and the fruit of godly "right" thinking.

Chapter 10

Receiving Godly Directions

One of the most important desires that God has for His people is that they receive direction from Him. Clear direction takes you to the right place at the right time and is guaranteed to bring right results. And that is "good."

But wrong directions take you to the wrong place at the wrong time and guarantee evil (contrary to God) results.

It is amazing to me at how many people will follow a man who is not going anywhere. If you follow a man who is not going anywhere, guess where you will end up? Nowhere.

Receiving directions from God is so important, but it was lost to mankind back in the Garden at the tree of knowledge of good and evil. For centuries, people have been trying to receive God's direction back. Others just don't care; they seem to be satisfied with making up their own minds about how life is to go.

So many sermons have been preached on how to hear the voice of the Lord. For me, I just didn't want to use the word "voice" because we very seldom hear from God in that manner. There have been many times when God speaks words to people, but I believe that **there are other ways of communicating that God practices for giving His direction.**

God Speaks Through Silence

One way He might communicate is in **complete silence.** God could be saying, "It's your call, but I may not be in it." You didn't hear anything, but you didn't feel anything either—seemingly, just no God involvement. It might be because it is a direction that He doesn't want for you, or it is the wrong timing, or He has already spoken about the direction before and He is not going to repeat Himself. Whatever the reason, with the silence should come a big red flag of caution.

Many, when they think that God hasn't spoken, assume He doesn't care or that it becomes okay to go that direction. Silence means silence with God. God is not saying anything, and that in itself says so much. Stop until you have confirmation that you are on the right path. Yes, that takes patience, and that is not so easy, especially when you need a fast decision. God knows the pressure that is on you, but it is better to slow down until you get His approval. The wrong choice can and will bring chaos, but patience has its own results. James tells us, "*But let patience have its perfect work, that you may be perfect and complete, lacking nothing*" (James 1:4).

I personally can't imagine that the God who loves us doesn't want to direct us. That would be like saying that God was pleased with man's choice back in the Garden, and He is looking for us to make up our own minds about life. Foolishness!

When you have no defined direction, don't do anything! By the way, that is "good" direction.

God Speaks Through Circumstances

Another way that God uses to communicate **is just circumstances**, the natural functions of life that might lead to the right direction for your future. Note how I said, "MIGHT lead to the right direction."

Psalm 37:23 says, "*The steps of a good man are ordered by the LORD, And He delights in his way.*"

The caution here is not to become a superstitious person and to start to read into everything that happens as if God is always sending you a sign through the circumstance of normal life. An example might be that a gust of wind blows a door shut, so you take it as if God said no.

Wow, how scary is that? The enemy could just cause something to take place, and you read into it and end up in the wrong place. That's why you need to know what is God and what isn't God. If you don't, then everything becomes a "sign" to lead you, and most of the time you will be misled. What are we doing following the natural to get into the spiritual? Yet I've seen so many do it over the years.

God Speaks Through Godly Counsel

Another way the Lord gives direction is a word from the counsel of a *well-respected* spiritual person.

I'm personally cautious about people who use the opening expression, "God told me...." I always think to myself that if God can tell them, then He can tell me personally. So I've learned over the years to wait on the Lord to hear the same thing. I won't move until I hear from God about it. And sometimes that will frustrate the people who gave me that "word," but it is my life, and the responsibility stops with me, so too bad!

Remember, David's men tried to convince him that it was God who brought King Saul into that cave so David could kill him. David even received a "word" from someone before it happened. So, as convincing it all appeared to be, David heard another voice on the inside that overrode human logic. Now, that's what I want in my life, and you should also.

We read about this voice in the life of Elijah:

> Then He said, "Go out, and stand on the mountain before the LORD." And behold, the LORD passed by, and a great and strong wind tore into the mountains and broke the rocks in pieces before the LORD, but the LORD was not in the wind; and after the wind an earthquake, but the LORD was not in the earthquake; and after the earthquake a fire, but the LORD was not in the fire; **and after the fire a still small voice.**

The most reliable expression of God's communication is His Word, the Bible.

God Speaks Through the Word

Now, here is the mature way to receive God's direction. I think that **the most reliable expression of God's communication is His Word, the Bible.** But even with that, I need to know the difference between reading a story and reading something that is directional for my life.

Again, we must ask if what we just read in the Bible is for direction now or just spiritual insight for edification? When the time comes and God is asking me to do something, don't you think that God would give clear direction? I do.

I can read about the faith of Abraham and how he truly moved with God because he knew that what he heard was from God for him. But if I move on what God told to Abraham, then I would be moving on what God told *him*, not on what God told *me*. My eyes are now off of God and on Abraham. I can desire the same results, but I won't get them because God wants to communicate direction directly to me. He has specific directions for me, for my best results, and for my life.

Also, the Bible expresses so much more than just His Word. It also expresses God's character, His nature, and His attributes. Combine all these with His Word and now you will have very good directions that you will know, and even feel in the goodness (glory) of His direction.

There is a peace or goodness that settles inside you that is unmistakable. Look for it, and don't settle for the peace of the flesh; you will find that won't last long. That is why being patient and giving direction the time it needs is so valuable. I call it **"the settling,"** it is as if God dropped, instantaneously, the approval for your direction.

Paul put it like this in Colossians 3:15: *"And let the peace of God rule in your hearts, to which also you were called in one body; and be thankful."*

I have received direction from God almost always with this verse in mind; with "the settling," you just know that you know. I never want to make a move without "the settling" in my heart, which is peace, but it can come fast, or it can take years.

God Is Not In A Rush

Here is a warning—there is very seldom a rush to God's direction. Why? Because God is in total control. If that is true, and you know it is, then take your time. The right direction for your life is worth your time. **Direction is always more important than time.** When you know that you know, then you move as fast as you want.

> God is in no hurry because He is in control.

God is in no hurry because He is in control. We are in a hurry because we want to be in control.

Time doesn't control God. If it did, then God would be subject to time instead of time being subject to God. The most powerful force on earth would be time and not God. I don't think He would let that happen.

When a situation that we don't have control of comes up, and we want to see it under control, we seem to be in a hurry. You know, the feelings arise that "it is now or never," or "It must be God because it fits exactly with my thinking and even my prayers." So we jump…only to find a future problem. Over the years I've seen so many people paint themselves into a corner, stopping their future, because of the decisions they made hastily.

I remember a time when we as a church needed to expand, and a new building was a big need on our minds. We looked everywhere to find a building. We thought about building our own, but being in San Bernardino with a growing church without much money, I just figured it didn't make much sense. So we continued to look for some type of available building. And sure enough, we found an old closed-down big box store. The size seemed okay—about 75,000 square feet. It was in an offbeat, dirty area of town.

We went to work trying to get it, and months went by without much progress.

Thirteen years later, I now can look back and see that the building would have been a noose around our necks and would have been much too small for what God had in our future. The building that we wanted would have stopped us from the future we desired and the future God desired.

We ended up building our own building on a piece of property that we looked at in the beginning of our search. This approximately 200,000 square foot building (under roof) has been such a blessing to us over the years!

As I write this, we are on the verge of paying off the entire property. How is this done with a people who don't have much money in a "no growth city" with one of the highest crime rates in the country? Again, this not about the people or the money; it is all about the great God who can do what He wants.

His pleasure brought His presence; His presence is all anyone needs. From His presence comes "the settling." We just need to find out what He wants, and that is not as hard as you may think.

God is not controlled by time because He controls time Himself. This very same God has placed time on your side in the decision-making process. He understands where we are coming from, the Garden. And He is in no hurry to see the flesh get directions for you.

One big reason that you do not want to be in a hurry is because often times God's direction doesn't make sense to us. So remember what James said and let patience have its perfect work.

Often His directions are just strange to our natural thinking.

The Bible is full of stories about people's lives and the directions they received from God that seem so difficult. Why is it that at times God requests of us to endure difficult times and things? Could it be that He just wants to show how much He is in control? **The more that we believe that He is in control, the more faith we will display** and the more we will react to His directions.

> The more that we believe that He is in control, the more faith we will display.

I remind you of Hebrews 11:6, which reminds us, *"But without faith it is impossible to please Him, for he who comes to God must believe that He is, and that He is a rewarder of those who diligently seek Him."*

Also, keep in mind that God's directions are not always weird. Most of the time they are just simple and practical to match His Word, character, nature, and attributes.

God Speaks Through Your Spouse

The last thing on how to receive spiritual direction that I think is important is that God can speak through your spiritual partner.

With me, it was my wonderful wife. Deby is an amazing minister of the Word of God. I respect her more than anyone I know. She has taught the Word of God around the world many times. When she would come home, she was always filled with new ideas and ways of doing things.

Most of the time, when I heard how others did their churches, I would listen but do nothing until I heard from God with the great release that He gives to us, "the settling." Then it was full-steam ahead, always building His Kingdom. I could trust her; I knew that she had His, and my, best interests in mind. But I moved very slowly.

Every day Deby and I start the day with God and coffee—a morning of brisk conversation about His Word or His people or His plan. It has become the best part of the whole day for me. Sometimes I'm sure that it had to be frustrating to her because it takes a long time for me to hear from God about her suggestions. I don't want to do something just because Deby thought it was great or I thought it was the right (good) thing to do.

I have become so dependent on God that I just had to get that "settling" from God on the inside. When I got it, the question of how or what was now all settled. The suggestions may not have been done right away, but it was complete (settled) in me.

An example is that when we were going to build our church, we hired the best construction company we could find. God had given His directions, and I was to follow. The company was to be big enough that this project was not the hallmark of their experience, yet they had to have some spiritual insight. It was settled in Deby and me.

We had very little money to complete this construction project. Because it was settled in us, we just kept going forward and carried a great peace. We never lost a night of sleep over it, and a year later we were doing what God would have us to do. Moving in and moving on. Settled!

Abraham should have listened to his wife Sarah about Isaac; life would have been a lot easier.

Chapter 11

Misplaced Trusts

We put our trust in so much. Think about it: people, man's word, money, the list can go on. If you have ever been let down by something that you thought was trustworthy, you know that is a painful experience and one that you never want to have happen again. I recently told my children that there are two things that you can count on in pastoring: one, you will be hurt over and over; and two, if you don't learn to handle it, you won't make it.

If you're any kind of a pastor, then you have believed in someone who didn't come through for you, and you were let down in a big way. We trust almost every day, most of the time in people or situations that we should not be putting our trust in. But we do. We have to; it is just part of the job. When we put our trust in something or someone, we leave ourselves open to great disappointments and hurts. It just goes along with the territory of the pastor.

With each hurt and every disappointment can come either a stumbling block or a starting block in the adventure of pastoring.

Misplaced trust, seemingly, is what happens in the lives of pastors. As I said, it will either be something that you stumble over or something that you stand on that makes you stand a little higher. It is up to you what you are going to do with disappointments.

In the life of Joseph, his relatives thought so little of him that they tried to kill him and then ended up selling him as a slave to a caravan on their way to Egypt. I would have been hurt, bitter, and disappointed beyond my imagination. Now a slave in a strange land with strange ways and among stranger people—how hurtful is that? All he ever knew was gone, and he was now facing a new world by himself.

Or was he?

You Have God and God Has You

> Joseph obviously had God, and God had him.

If Joseph was bitter or even greatly disappointed, you don't hear about it. He wasn't alone in his pain of disappointments; Joseph obviously had God, and God had him. In this, he could keep going forward until circumstance changed. And like him, you and I will have to learn that we are not alone in the times of disappointment of misplaced trust. Learning may take a lot of time for most pastors. Many times pastors feel so alone, with no one to talk to, no one to share their hurts with. But we all forget at times that we truly have God, and we are not alone. And it is in Him that we can go forward.

I sometimes think of Paul, this great apostle, when he was imprisoned or under house arrest for years. I see no place in the scriptures where his contemporaries, namely Peter, James, or John, came to comfort him in his time of need. You will even find people who wanted him dead and were fasting until someone killed him! How disappointing must that time have been, and you don't hear him complaining about it on any grand scale. Why? He had God, and God had him.

Here is a principle that took me years to learn but saved our ministry—even Jesus did not put His trust in man; He put his trust in the Father. John 2:24-25 says, *"But Jesus did not commit Himself to them, because He knew all men, and had no need that anyone should testify of man, for He knew what was in man."*

So over the years, I've learned that trust and love are two different things. God commands me to love the people, but I, like Jesus, put my trust in the Father. This keeps my relationship with people on the right plane. I love them, but I do not trust in them but in God. Most of us learn this lesson the hard way. The hard way just hurts over and over until you and I learn to love but to be cautious about where our trust goes.

I've learned to teach myself that it all will be okay—in fact, better than it was before. How could that be? Romans 8:28 says, *"And we know that all things work together for good to those who love God, to those who are the called according to His purpose."*

When we hurt because of misplaced trust, that's when we learn how to forgive. We have all done the right thing for people. Don't ever stop. And over and over we have been disappointed because we had to start over again. This, my friend, often times caused us to want to just give up. But, like our Jesus, we must learn to keep going forward.

Could there have been a deeper pain than David's experience with King Saul? He was so accepted at one time and so rejected just a few moments later! In just a few chapters, he loses Jonathan, his dear friend, and can no longer go to him for help. In a few verses, he loses Michel, his wife, and can no longer go to her and be with her. Then he loses his mentor, Samuel, and it is not safe to be with him. One moment his position was exalted in King Saul's kingdom. The next thing he sees is his name dragged through the mud.

The worst loss to most men is the loss of our own self-esteem, and David finds himself in the kingdom of his enemy, Achish, the King of Gath, in Goliath's hometown, begging and lying for a place to stay.

It would seem that every crutch he had to lean on was removed. How painful is that? The same thing will happen to you and me if we foolishly put our trust in man or money or fortune or fame.

Proverbs 3:5-6 tells us, "*Trust in the LORD **with all your heart, And lean not on your own understanding; in all your ways acknowledge Him, And He shall direct your paths.***"

Don't wait for the pain of misplaced trust to teach you the lesson. Learn now that your trust must be in Jesus and Him alone. Speaking of "alone," you are in this alone with Him. What more could you ask for?

Don't misunderstand—I'm not saying that you can't have friends. Just make sure that your trust is in your Jesus. Love and respect your friends, but there is one who sticks closer than a brother. His name is Jesus, and we can put all our trust and confidence in Him.

Chapter 12

The Wealth of the Poor

In Matthew 26:11 Jesus tells us, *"For you have the poor with you always, but Me you do not have always."*

I found over the years that if I take care of the poor, God will take care of me—and my church. That is not my heartbeat, but it is His. So again, how I feel has little to do with it. What He wants has everything to do with how I live my life.

> I found over the years that if I take care of the poor, God will take care of me—and my church.

Some years back, when the church was only a couple of hundred people, my wonderful wife told me that we needed to start thinking of the poor. She had this great burden for the people who didn't have much. My answer to her was "They can come to church if they want."

I, like so many others, was completely out of touch with the heart of God for the poor. Even though I may have good company in my thinking, I was still so wrong. If the truth be known, I just didn't care. I had enough to do by trying to hold my head above the water and keep on swimming, let alone taking on the needs of the poor.

"What can we do at this time?" I asked. "Maybe later as the church grows and we have some extra money," I said. She didn't argue with me, for she knew we didn't have any money to do anything like taking on the cost of the poor.

Sometime later, Deby, who has a heart for others more than herself, asked if she could use my little old pickup truck. She had a plan. She was going to get a big sack of dried beans and a big sack of rice from her own money. Then she would get a couple of girls from the church to help her put the dried beans and rice in smaller bags. Then they would go into San Bernardino, the poorest city in Southern California, and just go from apartment to apartment asking if anyone needed some food. And then she would explain that they only have beans and rice.

Almost every place she went welcomed this white woman's offer.

At first, I was so hesitant. This was not a safe city for this little white girl to be in, let alone going door to door. But I knew there was no stopping her. So I put a big life insurance policy on her (I'm kidding).

I'm so grateful for a truly godly wife. Over the years of watching her life, I've asked God many times if I'm even saved. One time I thought I heard Him say, "Did you really think you were?" But I'm sure He was just playing with me...I hope?

Everywhere Deby went, she just fell deeper and deeper in love with the poor. Each time she would ask me to go along with her and the girls, but I had an excuse; after all, I'm a pastor.

I remember when she started going to a cemetery to distribute food. I know that sounds funny, but she found that the homeless lived there because they could get water to drink and the grass was somewhat comfortable to sleep on. There she found families, lots of them with their little children, all living in a cemetery. Each week she became a friendly face that brought extra food and, of course, encouragement to all.

One family she became friends with had four small children. Mom and dad lived in the cemetery, they were not married but lived together for the last ten or so years. Deby got them to come to church; I think she picked them up and then arranged for others to pick them up. The whole family came right out of the cemetery.

Think about what God was saying—come from a place of death to a place of life. To this day, this is a picture of our church.

Bus Ministry

That is how the food distribution ministry started. And from this came our bus ministry. After Deby got to know the people and the people started to trust her, she would invite the people to church. But these people were truly poor and had no transportation to get to church. They could take the bus but had no money for the fare. So in order to get them to church, we would have to pick them up. But with what? We were hardly paying our bills and when we paid them, there is no money left over to buy or to even rent a bus. But keep in mind that when God is in something, something just happens in your heart.

Deby's passion was for the poor, and it still is. I kept on telling her that I was "the poor" in her life—if she just checked out my wallet, she'd find a big *zero* in it.

Then one day she pushed my passion button. It wasn't for the poor or the needy. She said to me, "It is too bad that we can't buy a bus, because I could fill it." BING! The light came on. I asked how many people was she talking about? She said around fifty. Fifty? At that moment I started to get a heart for the poor and the needy because fifty represented a 20% increase in attendance at our church with the first busload. Now that's called "church growth." As you can see, one is very spiritual and one is very carnal—guess which is which?

The very next week, I start to look for a bus—still with no money but with a new passion, not yet for the poor and needy but for church growth. From that moment, busses became a priority. I even carried pictures of busses in my wallet. My children were not happy about that because I didn't have pictures of them in my wallet, just busses.

It wasn't long before we bought our first bus. Then the other busses just came as the people caught the vision of the need to take care of the poor and the needy.

At first, having the poor and the needy in our church created lots of new challenges and even some big problems. Some of the people who came to our church didn't want to be around the poor and the needy and didn't want their children around them either. Yes, it is true, along with the poor and the needy come their problems.

There was an older couple who were members of our church and were also the biggest givers in the church. They came to us and told us they were leaving because they just didn't like having to deal with the poor people and wanted a church they could go to and not be bothered. It is always sad when people leave your church, so I've been sad for many, many years because there are always people who are leaving. However, even though these people left, God still provided—and in fact, we continued to grow and help even more poor people.

It became obvious that we needed some rules for the church and for the people coming in on our buses. These rules were mostly about manners and church etiquette. The church recognized that taking care of the poor was truly a God thing, and God loved our church for taking care of people.

Feed My Sheep

Today our church provides about 500,000 people each year with almost all their groceries, and we freely supply about fifty other churches and ministries with all the food that they give away. We even supply food to our local food banks! Now that's a food bill. It is all given for free and with no strings attached to the people in need. That is the heart of God. Most of the people we feed don't even go to our church. Someone once asked me why we would feed people who don't go to our church. My answer was simple: because God goes to this church, and He comes because we take care of the poor and needy.

God didn't bring the people into church because we provide them with all of their groceries. But better yet, God comes to our church because we feed the poor and show His manifested goodness to all. When God's presence is in your church, there is life; and where there is life, there is growth.

The Masses

The principle works like this—**if you don't take care of the messes, you'll never be trusted with the masses** (I heard someone say that).

> If you don't take care of the messes, you'll never be trusted with the masses.

David finds himself in a cave—depressed, rejected, and tired of running for his life—when God sends him some people. Rich and wonderful people? No, the low-lifers of Israel, maybe just to see what he was going to do with them.

We read in 1 Samuel 22:2, *"And everyone who was in distress, everyone who was in debt, and everyone who was discontented gathered to him. So he became captain over them. And there were about four hundred men with him."*

Just the fact that David runs to a cave says so much. Have you ever been in a cave? They are dark and often cold; weather and noise are out of the picture. He is alone, running for his life. He himself had to be down and discouraged, with a "just leave me alone attitude," I'm sure. And God sends to him people that have the same attitude—down, discouraged, running for their lives like him. They lost their homes and their farms, owed a great amount of taxes to King Saul, and went from a peaceful life to one of running.

Now, stop and think about it. If I was in this cave, running for my life, had just lost my future, was frustrated to no end and thought of as the "mess of Israel" and these losers come to me, I would have told them to go find their own cave and just leave me alone. I've got my own problems. But not David; he has every excuse, but doesn't use them. God had to be pleased with a man who takes on the cares of others **more than his own cares.**

Jesus Identifies with the Poor

Over the years, I have heard many pastors say to me that they just don't have the poor in their town and this type of ministry wouldn't work for them. So they proceed to tell me what they are doing, which is all fine and I'm sure it pleases God. But God is still into the poor, and you just can't get away from it. I'm not trying to judge anyone, but I'm trying to make a point. There are poor everywhere, but in some communities you have to go out and look for them. There are not a lot of people who look for the problems of the poor. Why should they? There are enough problems in ministry without the poor. I understand how they feel and even want to agree with them, but Jesus spends a lot of time talking about the poor and needy. But maybe those words are just for His time because times have changed? I don't think so, because *"the poor you will have with you always."*

I often say to these pastors that it's great that they are doing something for God. Then I tell them that there are poor people in the next town just a few miles away—lots of them! Truth be known, we American pastors love to build our churches in the path of growth—you know, the "suburbs." That's a place away from the down and out of our society. We like the new towns with new people in new houses; the nice people. I also agree that churches need to be built in the nice part of our towns. God wants the rich and famous, the comfortable and the clean, to have great pastors also—just not at the exclusion of the poor.

Many say to me, "I just don't have a heart for the poor." Well, I don't either, but I do have a heart for *God*. David was so special to God because "he was a man after God's own heart." Not after his own heart wants or feelings, but after God's heart. And His heart is after the poor.

Paul writes in 1 Timothy 6:17-19,

> *Command those who are rich in this present age not to be haughty, **nor to trust in uncertain riches** but in the living God, **who gives us richly all things to enjoy. Let them do good, that they be rich in good works, ready to give, willing to share,** storing up for themselves a good foundation for the time to come, that they may lay hold on eternal life.*

In Matthew 25:33-46, Jesus says these words:

*And He will set the sheep on His right hand, but the goats on the left. Then the King will say to those on His right hand, 'Come, you blessed of My Father, inherit the kingdom prepared for you from the foundation of the world: for I was hungry and **you gave Me food**; I was thirsty and you gave Me drink; I was a stranger and you took Me in; I was naked and you clothed Me; I was sick and you visited Me; I was in prison and you came to Me.'*

Then the righteous will answer Him, saying, 'Lord, when did we see You hungry and feed You, or thirsty and give You drink? When did we see You a stranger and take You in, or naked and clothe You? Or when did we see You sick, or in prison, and come to You?'

And the King will answer and say to them, 'Assuredly, I say to you, inasmuch as you did it to one of the least of these My brethren, you did it to Me.' Then He will also say to those on the left hand, 'Depart from Me, you cursed, into the everlasting fire prepared for the devil and his angels: for I was hungry and you gave Me no food; I was thirsty and you gave Me no drink; I was a stranger and you did not take Me in, naked and you did not clothe Me, sick and in prison and you did not visit Me.' Then they also will answer Him, saying, 'Lord, when did we see You hungry or thirsty or a stranger or naked or sick or in prison, and did not minister to You?' Then He will answer them, saying, 'Assuredly, I say to you, inasmuch as you did not do it to one of the least of these, you did not do it to Me.' And these will go away into everlasting punishment, but the righteous into eternal life.

Jesus identifies with the poor.

I don't want to be an irritant to these wonderful pastors, but I wanted to learn, so I kept on asking questions. Do you reach out to the prisons and prisoners? They and their families are very poor. Have you thought about the local convalescent hospitals? They are filled with poor older people. They always have needs. Most convalescent people never even get a visit. Or how about starting a food warehouse that gives to other ministries and they distribute to their poor or just those in need?

I've become abrasive to these pastors and have over the years lost many friends. Who knows, maybe I didn't really have those friends to start with. God forgive me, for the poor have become one of my passions now. I see the fruit of the effort that pays off big time in people's lives.

Many of these wonderful pastors would reply that they give through missions, and I think that is great. All churches should have a missions program, but don't stop there. If you can make it a personal ministry, operate within your church so the people can get involved, and they will feel satisfied. By the way, when people get involved and are satisfied (because they are doing the work of the ministry, Eph. 4:12), they tend to stay in your church longer. And they tell people how great your church is.

Another fun thing I found out is people with the money come to a church that is doing something. Yes, even if the church is filled with poor people. Often I will see the poor worshipping next to the rich; one came off the street not very long ago, and one just came from Wall Street. How pleasing to God this must be!

When you care for the poor, then God cares for you. The other day I was in the food lines at our church where thousands upon thousands come for their food. The number of hurting people was so overwhelming to me. There in front of everyone, I started to cry. Not wanting anyone to see my tears, I started to wipe fast, but the tears were faster than my hands. Then God spoke to me. He said, "This church will never fail and will continue to grow." My impression was that because we are doing a "good" job in taking care of the poor, He will sustain the church.

I just knew it wasn't the great preaching of the house or the great youth programs or even the 3,500 children that come to church here each week. It wasn't the LED screens or the smoke and lights that pleased God. That is all okay, but caring for the poor caught His attention. **True worship comes from "sacrificial obedience."** Sacrificial obedience brings great blessings, and great blessings make me cry.

The misjudgment of the poor has caused many churches the loss of His presence and the great loss of His pleasure, and that is a painful shame. I urge you, do not forget the poor.

Chapter 13

Falling in Love with Inadequacy

We all live in this world of inadequacy. Every day, all day. Most pastors see more of what we can't do and what we don't have than what we can do and could have. And because we do this, our thinking often stops us before we start. How much in life could have been accomplished if we never had to deal with the feelings of inadequacy and if we could truly feel we could accomplish anything?

> Most pastors see more of what we can't do and what we don't have than what we can do and could have.

As we said in chapter nine, World of Wrong Thinking, if the enemy can just get your thinking off the truth and get you to think wrongly about yourself, he will defeat you before you even start. You'll wonder, "Why start?" And you won't.

This is where we find out what we're made of. Are you just flesh and blood, or is your makeup body, soul, and spirit?

When I was a young person and had some idea that it could be the will of God for me to be in some form of ministry, I started wondering how could this be. I had never even read the Bible all the way through. Truth be known, I always tried to hide that I never read a book. No, not even one. In fact, my ability to read (as I mentioned before) was at a fifth-grade reading level. In school, I was the laughing stock of the classroom. I was very embarrassed about reading and any ability to be educated.

At the age of twenty, I got a job as a salesman with 3M Company in their adhesive tape division. I could sell and did it well. I still wasn't a Christian, and I thought life was all up to me. But after failure after failure in the business world, I finally came to Jesus with very little to offer.

Why would or how could Jesus want to use me? I had nothing to offer. Nothing! At this point, I became a willing person to *His* wants. At least I thought so—but like all of us, what we think and what we do are two very different things.

I started to look at my gifting, my talent, my abilities, and even any intelligence that I may possess to see what that was that God might want from me. That was a big mistake because God is not looking at anything that we think could be important. God did have a requirement of me, but it was not like anything I thought I could offer. God required me to take my inadequacy and surrender it to His adequacy.

I can't, and because I can't—He can. Crazy, I know (back to the Garden thinking).

Or, let's put it this way: I put in the natural and He puts in the super, and I now I have a supernatural experience.

Our Willingness, His Ability

So it was not about how smart I was or how educated I was or any of the things that we think we need to be in order to fulfill His will or plan. It is really about a person who comes to the conclusion, **all we will ever need is His ability.**

Don't misunderstand—I'm not saying that you don't need an education or some gifting. I'm saying it is all found in His ability to get you where you need to be. David

> All we will ever need is His ability.

didn't go to "king school" to learn how to be a king, but he did go to "heart" school and learn how to please God. We get educated and gifted in God's process, and He will help you to become what He wants. It's not what you think or you can do but what *He* can do in you and through you.

I could be very educated but not very smart. What I mean by that is I could learn how to read and learn how to take tests until I become the apex of academia and still be as dumb as a sack of rocks. It is God who takes us through the education process, teaching us what we need and causing us to understand what He wants to use in a life with Him. Why? Because each of us is different. Where you do not need to be trained, someone else may need lots of training; the opposite is also true.

Grace

Here is what I found to be true: **recognizing my inadequacy is the first step to His fulfillment of my life's desire.**

Isn't that what grace is all about? For years we've defined grace as "unmerited favor." This is true, but few of us truly understand what that means because we don't talk that way anymore. We don't understand the fullness of the word "unmerited" or even "favor." It means that God gives you something that you didn't earn, but it means so much more. It is saying that God's ability comes in when your ability can't go any further.

I taught our church this little statement: "**Grace is God's sovereign, divine ability to get the job done on my behalf when I can't do it.**" Now that is grace.

Deby put it much simpler. She says," **Grace is God's power in me to do what God's Word demands of me.**"

With all of that in mind, let's look at some Scriptures.

Paul writes in 2 Corinthians 12:7-11:

> *And lest I should be exalted above measure by the abundance of the revelations, a thorn in the flesh was given to me, a messenger of Satan to buffet me, lest I be exalted above measure. Concerning this thing I pleaded with the Lord three times that it might depart from me. And He said to me, "My* *grace is sufficient for you, for My strength is made perfect in weakness." Therefore most gladly I will rather boast in my infirmities, **that the power of Christ may rest upon me.***

> *Therefore I take pleasure in infirmities, in reproaches, in needs, in persecutions, in distresses, for Christ's sake. **For when I am weak, then I am strong.** I have become a fool in boasting; you have compelled me. For I ought to have been commended by you; for in nothing was I behind the most eminent apostles, though I am nothing.*

Note in verse seven, it is not about Paul and what he has and or what he carries. To prove that, God allows a messenger of Satan to come against him. This keeps him dependent on God (be mindful that "dependency" is "humility").

He asked God three times to remove the condition. To me, when Paul, this great apostle, asks God for something and doesn't get it, we should pay close attention. God did not remove the problem (God does not always answer our prayers because He wants us to see something).

This statement says it all. Not only for Paul but also for you and me: "My grace **[God's sovereign divine ability to get the job done on our behalf when we can't do it]** is sufficient for you, for My strength is made perfect in your inadequacy" (my paraphrased version).

In verse ten through eleven, Paul talks about his feelings, and these feelings should be our feelings because we should understand the importance **the role of our inadequacy plays.**

In James 4:6 it says, "*But He gives more grace. Therefore He says:* "*God resists the proud, But gives grace to the humble.*"

And in 1 Corinthians 1:27 Paul says, "*But God has chosen the foolish things of the world to put to shame the wise, and God has chosen the weak things of the world to put to shame the things which are mighty.*"

My failures and lack of ability to get things accomplished is an accepted position to God, and not a bad thing, because in my weakness and lack of ability, then He is made strong. When you recognize this, you and God are now in your proper roles in order to accomplish His will. This now becomes the exact position that God wants mankind to be in—completely

> We do the best we can, but our confidence is in what He can and will do.

dependent on Him for all fulfillment as we were before the fall or before the tree of knowledge of good and evil.

Here is a fun question: "In your future, who needs to be strong—you or God?" The answer may surprise you. The answer is "both." We do the best we can, but our confidence is in what He can and will do. That is the kind of thinking that takes a church of hundreds to a church of thousands.

I know that I have no answers to life, but I know the One who has all the answers to everything. And because I'm humble, "dependent," He will add His ability to fulfill His plan for me.

Made Strong

There are many fascinating verses in Hebrews eleven. I find verse thirty-four very interesting. This verse talks about all the great people of Hebrews eleven where no names are mentioned. It is saying something great about these people that we need to see. It is the very thing that makes them special enough to be in the Bible.

It says they "quenched the violence of fire, escaped the edge of the sword, **out of weakness were made strong**, became valiant in battle, turned to flight the armies of the aliens" (Hebrews 11:34).

Their "faith" was simply dependency on God—humility.

So fall in love with the plan of God and realize that your inadequacy is the open door to His power that will fulfill His plan for your life. We all understand this, we minister this, but we forget it, and we live very troubled lives.

God gets the job done for us in our weakness. That's why the Bible says, *"All things are possible to him that believes."* Believes in what? In a God that gives more grace to the humble or dependent.

Chapter 14

The Supreme Power of the Universe

God's love is the supreme power of the universe.

So many times, we pastors forget the truth about how much God loves His people. Without an emphasis of this in our ministries, we fall short in our jobs to the Lord. Sometimes we will treat the people as if they are in our churches for *our* sakes instead of us being there for *their* sake. When you mess with what God loves the most, you will become a person that is in trouble. A non-pleasing person receives very little from God.

God's love is the supreme power of the universe.

God always loves us, but that does not mean that He always approves of what we do and the motives behind how we act. Love and approval are two very different things, and we should not get them mixed up.

If you and I don't watch out for how we treat this understanding, we won't last long.

Ezekiel 34:11-12 says, *"For thus says the Lord GOD: 'Indeed I Myself will search for My sheep and seek them out. As a shepherd seeks out his flock on the day he is among his scattered sheep, so will I seek out* **My sheep and deliver them from all the places where they were scattered on a cloudy and dark day.'"**

Understanding God's love for His people will cause us to fulfill His plans for His church.

Everyone talks about love and how much God loves us. We have all taught it so many times that we are convinced we completely understand it. So when I start to talk about the subject of love, immediately some pastors start to turn off. Why? Because we have all taught about it so much that it must be impossible that there could be something that we missed.

Even so, try to stay with me. In some circles, this is a boring and blasé message; don't let it be. Love is not a new subject—we just need a new and fresh understanding of its depth of importance.

God *Really* Loves His People

We all know that God so loved the world that He gave His only begotten Son, we know that God *is* love, and we know that God loves His people. That is why it is so much more than a God who loves His people; it is about God who *really* loves His people. *Really!* To the place where we come to see that the God of the Bible expresses more about the love He has for His people than He expresses about who He is.

Someone once said to me that the Bible is all about God and everything in it is about God. But it is about a lot more; it is about the love and desire that God has for His people. In fact, *"God is love,"* so everything He is expresses His love towards His people. This kind of love is beyond our natural thinking but must play a giant role in how we conduct ourselves as pastors and followshippers.

Without an idea of the depth of love that God has for His people, our leadership activities will only be directed by our thinking and by our limited evaluations. This in turn will keep us at much lower-level Christian labors.

When we see parents today who don't show the proper care for their children, we usually see these children not developing to their full potential. It is the same with our churches today. The care for His children, for the most part, is trusted to the care of His leadership (or should I say "followship"). As the leadership goes, so goes the development of His most important love, His people. Wow, this is a serious matter, and God takes it very serious. So should we.

You Are There for Them

For many years, I was involved in things that were important to *me*. I sincerely thought that how I felt and what I did had to be pleasing to God. But it wasn't. I watched other churches to see what was important to them and took my directions, often times, from them. After all, there seemingly is comfort and safety in numbers. They seemed to be working on some basic areas of their ministry that I, of course, picked up on. You know, the guy with the largest church is the most spiritual or the one that has the nicest building or has the most money. When all that translates to ministry, it becomes about me and not about what God really wants for His love—His people.

The people can become the pawns in the game of church that we use to further our selfish ambition and our feelings, when I should be concerned about where and what the people should be doing in order for God's development. It can all become about me, and I can use the people for my personal gain—all because I don't understand the depth of God's love for them, not just for me. Truth be known, for years I was in church for me, and not in church for them. I saw them as being there for me. How messed up is that?

Please don't misunderstand—having a nice building and lots of people with lots of money is not ungodly. It is a "good" thing, a God thing. But if that becomes your goal to achieve, then that level of ministry has missed the most important desire that God has for His people and His love.

Over the years I have seen many occasions where the pastor was ungodly in his lifestyle, and it was no secret; the whole church knew about the pastor's sins. The surprise came when the church stayed together and did not fall apart. I questioned God. How can it be that this pastor and his sin, which are seen by all, seemed to be overlooked? I found myself frustrated with God, but then the answer came and filled my heart with joy. His answer was, "I love my people more than your desire for punishment of the pastor. To scatter the flock without a healthy pasture for them will only bring harm to My love, the people." But I cried out, "What about that pastor?" God did not answer, but down the road, God dealt with him His way.

God's Love Started in the Garden

How do I start to see the love that God has for His people? It all starts in the Garden. Right from the beginning, we see His love and His desire for them.

God makes a statement about them—sometimes God says so much without saying anything; He speaks often by what He *does*. In the beginning, God established His desire for His people—to bless them in every area of their lives—and from that day to this, His desire has not changed. His desire for His love, His people, is to prosper them in every arena of life.

You might say, "How do you know that?" It is so simple and simply overlooked. God creates and places them in a garden. God could have placed them anywhere, but He desired a garden—not a dump or in a state of poverty or even a desert. No, Eden was a garden with everything that they could ever want or need, including His personal guidance. We can only imagine the comfort and the smells, the temperature, and the peace beyond our understanding. Truly, it was the most beautiful piece of land that the earth ever carried—all for His love, His people. How much does that say without God speaking a word?

Life in the Garden is what God wants for His people. He wants to bring the love of God, His people, to a place of comfort and peace, where they can once again receive direction from Him because He is the ultimate leader that will lead them to their personal promised land.

God Loves His Sheep

I can only imagine what God saw and felt when He looked and saw how young David was taking care of his father's sheep on the hills of Judea. As you know, at times God will refer to His people as sheep. David had great concern for his father's sheep. Even after he was anointed by the great Samuel to be king, he went back to the sheep, fought for them, even put his life on the line for them. Just dirty sheep of no real value. Wow!

Sometimes we have people in our churches who seem of no value. They don't dress very well or they don't have many teeth in their mouth. Maybe they are not very well-educated or have no important job. They can't give or even contribute much at all. What does God see? Someone of great value, a very important person, someone who has great potential because it is God in them that makes up for everything the world took out of them. We may be seen as losers to the world, but God sees us differently.

Value for anything is determined by what someone might pay for it. An example: A piece of artwork has a value placed on it that is established because of what someone paid for it. If it is a small amount, then the picture is not very valuable. But if someone will pay a great amount for it, then the value is great.

The value of God's people can only be determined by the price Someone paid for it. There is only one price that has ever been paid for humanity. It wasn't with gold, silver, or even diamonds. No, not even a planet or a solar system. For God loves His people so much that He paid the highest price He could for them, Himself, as He breaks from His side and sends His only begotten Son.

I think we all understand that. But what about the people who are a pain to your life? It is wrong to think that we only get the troubled ones, but, of course, it always seems like the other pastors got the easy ones. But you know that is not true.

In 1 Peter 2:9-10 we read,

But you are a chosen generation, a royal priesthood, a holy nation, His own special people, that you may proclaim the *praises of Him who called you out of darkness into His marvelous light; **who once were not a people but are now the people of God,** who had not obtained mercy but now have obtained mercy.*

Paul writes, *"No temptation has overtaken you except such as is common to man; but God is faithful, who will not allow you to be tempted beyond what you are able, **but with the temptation will also make the way of escape, that you may be able to bear it"*** (1 Corinthians 10:13).

Sometimes when you are troubled by people and someone gives you a Scripture, it doesn't feel very good. I'd much rather hear that everyone has as much trouble as me—and maybe more. Now, that feels good! But the truth is, some can handle it and others can't. The way of escape is always the same. It is not when the problem people leave or we get rid of the problem; it's when you and I connect with God about that problem. That is the way of escape.

It is not about what we think of these people; it is about what *He* thinks of His people. And He loves them, messed up or not. He loves them and is waiting for someone to treat them as if they are the most important commodities on the earth. And truly, they are.

The Power Is Love

This is not to say that you put up with the ungodliness of these people. We forget that God has not called us to be their punching bag but has called us to be their pastor. Sometimes I need to be stern with some of the people of God. Blunt might be another word for it. I'm not out to harm them, but I'm out to get them away from their ungodliness, which will bring them devastation.

Remember the sheep stuck in the mud that my family rescued. It wasn't there because it was following; it was stuck because it made a bad choice.

The call is to shepherd them to green pastures—if they will let you. If not, then talk to God about it, and He will give you direction. Sometimes God will release them to a pastor that they might respect more. Don't see it as something bad about you but something good about them. That is what the rod and staff are for—to guide, comfort, and correct. Correction is not always fun but very necessary.

When someone left our church, I always took it personally, and for days I would be discouraged. So I got in the habit of asking God for ten more to replace them. Maybe that is why the church got so big! Lots and lots of God's people have left and broke my heart. But I learned to find my comfort in Him; He is always with us (Psalm 23:4).

So no matter who they are or how they act, we as leaders must see them as God's greatest commodity on the earth, because He died that they may live.

Remember, God's love is the supreme power of the universe, because it cannot fail. In 1 Corinthians 13:8, Paul writes, "**Love never fails**. *But whether there are prophecies, they will fail; whether there are tongues, they will cease; whether there is knowledge, it will vanish away.*"

Always implement His power—love. You might say to yourself, "How do I do that?" For me, I had to remember that I was a servant. Here is where there can be some confusion at times. Yes, I am a "servant." A servant is a servant to his master, so being a pastor, I become a servant of God. We sometimes see ourselves as servants of *the people*, but truth be known, I am not a servant of the people except through the direction of our Master. I am a servant to the Master's will and plan for His people. If I try to become a servant to the people, it can become an overwhelming job, and truly, some people will just drive you nuts. I used to become so frustrated that I would want to quit, and many pastors have.

This is going to sound crazy, but I don't always feel love for the people, but when I take on my Master's heart, I always fall in love with my Master's "love"—His people. What I do is not always because the people live up to my expectations or my standards, but **because I live up to His expectations and His standards.** Jesus is the Master whom I serve. I'm in love with Him, and He helps me as a servant to act out His love towards His people—"His love." Has God asked me to love His people? Yes; through Christ I love His people.

Think about this—when Moses stopped becoming a servant of God and became the accuser of the people, he was kept out of the Promised Land. It is not about how much I love the people, but it is about how much I love my Master, who uses me to show His love to His people.

A servant must be obedient to His Master. Can you imagine a servant who questions everything his "boss" asks of him or ignores what he requests? It just does not work that way. I once had an employee who acted like that (notice how I said, I "once" had). A servant must have faith that the master knows what he is doing. A servant must be unselfish because it is all about what the master wants, not what we want.

> A pastor is a servant to the Master's will, and not a slave of His people.

A pastor is a servant to the Master's will, and not a slave of His people.

Last year, a person that I know, but don't really respect, came and visited me at our church. Truth be known, I don't think I even like this guy very much (shocking, how fleshly I can be). I'm just not in agreement with his ministry and have a hard time caring for him. In the middle of our annoying conversation, the Lord spoke to me about giving him a large sum of money. In my heart, I was saying to the Lord that the church can't afford to give this guy that kind of money— that's a lot. And then I clearly hear the Lord say, "I didn't ask the church to give it, but I did ask you to give it, from your own money, that I have given to you."

Before I knew it, I had my check book out and was writing him a check for a lot more money than I wanted to give. On the inside, I knew it was God; on the outside, I hated it. I didn't even like this man, and I was thinking that there was no way he would live up to any of my expectations.

Later that day when Deby and I were alone—she knew how I felt about this guy—she asked me why I did it. My response was, "Because God asked me to do it." It is easy to respond to those who make us happy or fulfill our expectations and standards. It's easy to respond to those people we like, but as a pastor, as a servant to the Master, we are going to have to show His love even to the hard to love—because the Master loves them all.

I leave you with this. Romans 5:8 tells us, "*But God demonstrates His own love toward us, in that while **we were still sinners**, Christ died for us.*"

Chapter 15

Strange Are Your Churches

Over the years, I've seen God work in the strangest places. What I mean is that God works in churches other than mine.

At first, I questioned God. "How can this be? They don't even know what they are doing, their doctrine is all messed up, and they live in routines and rituals. Why, there is hardly any teaching of the Word of God..."

It seemed to me that it was a gathering of people that just have some level of knowledge about God. Some of their leaders were people who had a high degree of education but seemed to be limited to the thinking of their movement or denomination and were therefore limited in what they understood.

I found myself full of my own thinking, prejudice, and judgments. I started to become the critic and the judge of God's church. Please let me point out that no one has the ministry of criticism and gossip. The only judgment I'm allowed is the judgment of what is spiritual.

The Apostle Paul wrote, "But the natural man does not receive the things of the Spirit of God, for they are foolishness to him; nor can he know them, because they are spiritually discerned" (1 Corinthians 2:14). The next verse reads, "*But he who is spiritual judges all things, yet he himself is rightly judged by no one*" (vs 15).

So I can judge all things that are spiritual, but not other people and their ministries. That is God's job, not mine, and when I go there, it makes me the judge of God and His ways. When I do that, I'm in trouble because that stops the growth of my church, and I've become very displeasing to God.

One day while teaching the Bible, God highlighted a verse in my heart. You know what that is like—the Word jumps off the page at you and stays with you. This is the verse: "*Who are you to judge another's servant? To his own master he stands or falls. Indeed, he will be made to stand, for God is able to make him stand*" (Romans 14:4).

God had made the statement clearly, and I had to adhere to it. I was in sin because I was questioning God and His methods. I pleaded guilty to the Lord.

In the days that followed, God spoke many things about my condition towards His church, most of which I wanted to disagree with but I knew to be true. The things that He spoke to me about were not very pleasant. He said, "You are a divider of my church; the very thing that you are called to unite, instead, you are causing division."

Wow, I felt horrible. Then I heard, "You hate my church. How could you love me and hate my church?"

Somewhere there is a lie going on, and it is in me, and stopping God's work toward building my own church. "*If someone says, "I love God," and hates his brother, he is a liar; for he who does not love his brother whom he has seen, how can he love God whom he has not seen?"* (1 John 4:20)

"How could this happen in me?" I asked. And He started to explain; He started in my past.

The Competition

When I was a young man, my parents brought me up in a mainline denomination. This denomination never taught me anything about the Word of God, only the rules of the church. I grew up not knowing anything about God except that He existed. So when I found out the truth about God from the Bible, I was blown away and very angry that this very large denomination had people trapped in the thinking of the church and not in the truth of what God had for them. I became a critic.

"How do I hate?" I asked.

God said, "You have made other churches your competition."

He was right. The enemy, to me, was other churches—especially the churches that were close to me. The churches that were far away I had no problem with—except for one thing, jealousy. I was a mess! A mess that God was going to clean up and use.

How could God ever use me? The answer to that is very simple—He loves His people more than my foolishness. Patiently, He was waiting for me to get my act together.

On the outside, I looked very spiritual and even said the right things. Surely no one would ever know what was dark and lurking on the inside. However, try to get away if you can, but there is no hiding from the One who sees the heart.

"Lord, what do I do?" I said. "I'm willing to change. What would you have me to do?" His answer was very strange: "Pray for their success." This wasn't an easy request of me, but I love Him, so when He asked me to do something, I did it, even though it was strange for me. I started to pray for their success. "No," He said. Then I heard, "Not in private, but in front of the whole church and on your knees, before each time that you teach." I was teaching about 300 times per year, having eleven church services per week. So the church heard this prayer each service.

Here is where the miracle comes in; I started to fall in love with other churches and stopped feeling that I was in competition. I had a new feeling of united faith for the churches over all. This doesn't mean that I had to get involved in the things that other churches were doing, like joint men's meetings, etc. I was busy doing what God would have our church to do, and other churches should be doing what God had them to do.

Wounds

How did I get so judgmental and critical?

When Deby and I were young and the church was smaller, we attended a great man of God's pastors' conference. I would guess there were about 2,500 attendees. In the very first service the speaker said, "Turn to the people around you, and shake hands and greet them." We stood, and the man and woman in front turned and looked at us. I put on a friendly smile and put out my hand to shake; they both stopped and turned abruptly from us and sat down. We both felt that was strange, but we just went on with the conference. The next day we moved to another part of the seats, and again the man on the platform said, "Turn around and greet the people around you." Sure enough, the same people were again in front of us. Again, they both turned away and sat down. We just shrugged our shoulders and sat back down. We had no idea what the heck was going on; we'd never seen these people in our lives. Later on in the conference, we found two seats together, and the speaker said the same thing. Sure enough, the same people were in front of us, and again they turned around and saw us and just kept on turning. Crazy, I thought.

The conference ended, and I thought no more about it—until a few months later when this man came by my office at the church. I remember the timing because we were so broke that my office had butcher paper on the windows used for makeshift window coverings. I recognized that it was the very same man who acted so strange at the conference. He asked if we could talk, so we sat and talked.

Then I heard something very important. He introduced himself as a pastor of a small denominational church across town. He was not only the pastor but also the regional director for his denomination for that entire area. Wow, I was without words at this point. I wondered how a pastor and a great leader of other churches could treat people he didn't even know like he treated us. He explained that people had been leaving his church for ours for years now, and he had come to the place where he just hated us because we had ruined his life. I stopped him and said, "I don't even know you." "Yes," he said, "But I made it a point to know *you*." He believed that it wasn't a mistake that he and his wife kept turning around to find us at the conference; they were being confronted by God to deal with this issue once and for all. He asked me to forgive him for his foolishness. Of course, I forgave him, and we prayed and departed from each other.

He was free, but I wasn't. It really bothered me that someone who was a "man of God" could feel the way he did and treat people like he did. For me, this just started to reinforce the wall of division in my life.

Man of God

It really started years before in a little church that we started with just a hand full of people. We were pastoring about one hundred people in the small vacation town of Lake Arrowhead, California, where many people worked on weekends because of the number of people that came up to the mountain for weekend holidays. It was a hard place to pastor because the people seemed not to want any kind of deep relationship with God, and they seemed just to desire to work and play. A vacation mentality keeps people in a trap of playing.

After about a year, I had heard that there was a pastors' prayer meeting taking place at another church, and the pastors of the mountain were all going to be there. I was not invited; someone from my church just told me about it after Sunday service. I thought that if it is for pastors, then I should go. I was so looking forward to meeting and talking with other pastors. Wow, and to pray together, could life be any better?

It was a nice church, and I was surprised at the twenty-five or so pastors that showed up. We went around a circle introducing ourselves, and when it was my turn, I simply introduced myself. The place got silent, and they all stared at me. No one had ever met me, but they all heard about my little church. I just expected them to accept me and move on; after all, we are all Christian men, pastoring Christian churches, and most of these men were very highly educated by their denomination.

The first man that spoke was a man who had the largest church in the area and the education to back it. What he said would change me for the next twenty years of my life and would hinder the work of God in my life and church. He said out loud so all could hear, "I won't pray with this man; and if he won't leave, I will." I didn't know who he was talking to or about. I thought it couldn't be me. But it *was* me, and I was so embarrassed. This man was the most respected of all the pastors on that mountain.

I just sat there stunned, red-faced, with perspiration starting to run down my face. I had no idea what that was all about. Then one after another, the pastors stood up and followed him out. I was left all alone except for the pastor who hosted the event; if it wasn't at his church, maybe he might have left also. When I stood up to leave, he followed me out and told me of his disappointment in the others.

With tears in my eyes, I turned and asked, "Why?" His answer stunned me, "Maybe they are jealous, or just religious. I don't know." I wondered what they could possibly be jealous of. And "religious," what does that mean? I was so new to this that I just didn't understand.

I got to my car and just sat there, stunned, and started to cry. I'm 6'5" tall and weigh 250 pounds, and I was crying like a baby. I cried all the way home and wanted to quit the ministry. I felt that I couldn't tell my wife what had happened. I may have been young and deeply hurt, but I was still a man. But eventually I had to tell Deby; she could see that something was wrong. When I told her, she felt deeply for me, and we cried for hours together.

I didn't know any other pastors to talk about this with, so I just held it inside for the next twenty years and started to build that wall of hate and mistrust. I now see that a so-called "man of God" can be as bad, and maybe even worse, than any businessman. This should not be; the "Word of God" must be the guideline for our actions.

I Like Me

For the many years that were to follow, it was no different. We went to meeting after meeting, and most of the time it was just a dislike for both my wife and me. I remember the time we were invited to an Inland Pastors Association meeting for the first time. When we questioned the motives of a decision that was being made, we were both asked to leave and never come back. We truly must have done something, but for the life of us, we had no idea what it was. We again just wanted to quit, but we didn't. We just moved on.

One time when our church had about 4,000 people, we again were asked to join a group of pastors in the Palm Springs area. We went not expecting much, just hoping to have some good healthy fellowship that we so needed, only to find a strange thing was about to happen.

We were all sitting around this large table with our wives. I would guess about twenty-five pastors and their wives. While the conversation was pleasant, out of nowhere a man across the table said out loud so that all could hear, "I'm glad I'm not you." He was obviously speaking to me even though we hadn't said a thing to each other during this whole meeting.

I thought to myself, here we go again, and I said, "I'm glad you are not me too; I like me." Everybody laughed to get past this awkward moment, and the meeting went on. After the meeting, Deby and I agreed that was very weird, but not uncommon for us. By now, the two of us had our guards up every time we were around other pastors. They were not our friends.

Escape the Trap

I had fallen into the trap—the same trap that the others were in, and only love could break its hold. Galatians 6:1 says, "*Brethren, if a man is overtaken in any trespass, you who are spiritual restore such a one in a spirit of gentleness, considering yourself lest you also be tempted.*"

When God intervened and asked me to pray for their success, I truly hated that idea—that's how I knew it was God! I no more wanted the success of these guys than I wanted everyone at our church to leave and go to theirs. But it was God.

By this point, the church had grown to about 24,000 members, and we were in our building that sat about 2,700 people. We were now a large church, and at the beginning of each service, we prayed for the success of our fellow churches. The prayer would contain a portion that defined who we were praying for. It might sound like this, "Lord, bless all the churches in the Inland Empire [our part of the LA area], and around the world, that are preaching the Gospel of our Lord and Savior Jesus Christ. They are our brothers and sisters. Bless the Baptists, Methodists, Presbyterians, Lutherans, and all the Protestant denominations and all of our Pentecostal and Evangelical churches, our Catholic and Adventist brothers and sisters." Then I would go on naming a few local churches by name. This whole prayer took about two minutes but turned out often to be the most powerful two minutes of our time together.

The prayer started to change not only me but also my church; the people started to see and feel the importance of unity. Other churches would hear that we as a church were praying for them by name, and fear and dislike were replaced with love and care. Respect without judgment was taking place in our hearts, and the spirit of competition was removed and a spirit of freedom and oneness was building.

When pastors heard this, it gave them the freedom to start to pray for other churches in their area. Instead of being our competitors, they now became our companions in the building of His church, and this was the difference that is pleasing to God. In that security, God can and will grow His church.

In order for me to do this, I had to know that God wasn't against any of His churches. There was a church for everyone. Wherever the people were, God wanted to meet them there. What I mean by that is whether the people were traditional-minded or preferred a ritual type of a church, or if they liked a free expression type of church or maybe a teaching or a worshipping church, there was a church for them. I learned it was not my place to judge.

As long as they ministered the Gospel of our Lord Jesus, they were His responsibility. I'm free, and that makes me happy. The one thing that would keep me from blessing them would be if they have a doctrine that prevents people from being saved. It would be ungodly of me to bless them in their foolish expression and beliefs.

Please keep this in mind that I don't just have a free for all; I don't pray for all religions of the world. No way! My prayer is for brothers and sisters that are born again and are Christians. You can find them in all the different Christian churches.

Different Churches, Different Practices

Another thing that I had to come to terms with was that not all churches are the same in how they do services and even their understanding of the Scripture. Here is what I mean—can I misunderstand Scripture and still be born again and go to heaven? Of course, because eternal life doesn't come by *knowledge* but by a heartfelt *surrender* of all your life and all your heart to Jesus as your Lord and Savior, or being "born again" as Jesus said in John three.

If it were based on intelligence, then lots of people wouldn't make it, including me. Maturity, on the other hand, comes by knowledge, not salvation. Salvation comes by surrender to His Lordship as you invite Him into your life as Lord with all your heart and life. God extends grace, and faith receives it.

So a lot of churches conduct their services differently than we conduct ours. And that is okay. Why? Because it is His church, not my church.

Here is a big question—do I believe that we do church the best way that we could be doing church? Absolutely. But, the truth be known, so do the other churches, or else they wouldn't do it their way.

God, in all His wisdom, has created a church that meets the needs of everyone. How smart is our God! He knows what He is doing! He is in total control.

> God, in all His wisdom, has created a church that meets the needs for everyone.

There should never be anything between us except true care one for another. We read, *"For you are still carnal. For where there are envy, strife, and divisions among you, are you not carnal and behaving like mere men?"* (1 Corinthians 3:3)

A few times in our ministry, people from other churches have come to me and said that they were leaving their old church and wanted to know if there is a place for them here at this church. In my questioning of them, I would find out that they played a key role in their old church. Some, I found out, were excellent at what they did, and I would have loved to have them to be part of our church.

But if I hurt that other church because I want this person at my church, then God would hold me responsible for the loss of that other church.

Who has the desire to hurt other churches? Who would love to bring loss to a church? That is a demonic principle, and I would be judged for what I'd done that caused loss in another church. So I always made sure that they went back and talked to their pastors and tried to work out the differences. Then and only then could I receive these new people with good conscience.

Many times, I would not use a person coming from another church for a year just to see if they were really in tune with our church. Often times, I would follow up with the other pastor by giving them a call. I don't think I ever got a very good reception, and I can understand that because no one ever likes to lose people from their church.

I can only remember a couple of times when a pastor from another church called me to tell me that so and so was now attending their church. It's funny how over the years we have filled up so many of the churches around us with thousands of people that left us and ended up at other churches!

I found that a lot of pastors don't care if they hurt our church, and they just don't make any effort to prepare us for the loss of these people. It might be because when you have a lot of people, they don't feel sorry for you. But again, it is not about me; it is about God and what is best for His people.

Paul put it like this:

> *For when one says, "I am of Paul," and another, "I am of Apollos," are you not carnal? Who then is Paul, and who is Apollos, but ministers through whom you believed, as the Lord gave to each one? I planted, Apollos watered, but God gave the increase. So then neither he who plants is anything, nor he who waters, but God who gives the increase. Now he who plants and he who waters are one, and each one will receive his own reward according to his own labor. For we are God's fellow workers; you are God's field, you are God's building. According to the grace of God which was given to me, as a wise master builder I have laid the foundation, and another builds on it. **But let each one take heed how he builds on it.***

1 Corinthians 3:4-10

Every effort from every pastor must be taken to protect and guard our fellow Christian churches so that we, in our zeal, do not bring harm to them. If we do, it will stop church growth because our actions were not pleasing to God. The people that came today will not be the people that are here tomorrow. When people come to your church through human manipulation, they won't last long and will hurt your heart when they leave.

Do all that you can to see that they left their old church in a righteous manner. This is not easy for large churches, but if you hear of something, make sure that you or someone follows up. Do all you can to show other churches that you are not out for yourself and you care about them also.

Chapter 16

The Real Look Into Pastoral Ability

Sometimes we shoot ourselves in the foot by thinking that all people are alike. What one person does well may not even be in the thinking of another.

We see what is in the Bible, and we love it. But to most people who attend our churches, the Bible is just not that important to them. That is why some carry their Bibles and others come to church not carrying anything.

Over and over I've said, "Bring your Bible to church. And if you don't have one, I'll give you one. It is so important to learn what God has for you to live out." Unfortunately, most of the people don't listen.

In most churches, the first three or four rows of people are always in tune with you; it seems that they just want to learn and study the Word of God. The further back you go, the less interest they have. I have found that the higher the education, the better the attention seems to be. People who were easily distracted just have difficulty staying with you. Yet all of our churches are filled with people who are easily distracted.

Sometimes the 25% or so of our church that is attentive shapes the directions of our church. We seem to play to them and not the others, bypassing that large need of the majority.

Not everyone who comes to our churches wants to work in our church. They just want to sit and take in. And that is okay with God. It is not the best situation for them to be in, but it is the way it is. Can we change that position or must we just live with it?

Balance

I remember when I was a young Christian, I worked hard all week long with a lot of stress that went with my job. So when I went to church, I didn't want to work hard at something that I knew very little about; I just wanted to take in and enjoy the newly found freedom in Christ Jesus that was all so new and fresh to me. If someone put too much pressure on me, it may have run me off. Then what good is it if I'm no longer in church? It is a fine line trying to get the sheep to fertile pastures and not run them off in our enthusiasm for their health and well-being. It is a balancing act that takes a lot of practice to perfect.

Please hear me. I'm not saying that you should compromise your message. NO! Just don't expect everyone to yell "amen" when your point is made. Wherever people are at, it is my job to encourage them to a closer and deeper relationship with the King—even if they don't want it. It is in that relationship that they find the deep commitment into His service.

> A man will only go as far as he is encouraged to go.

A man will only go as far as he is encouraged to go.

I heard a story once and, I don't know if it is true, but it's a good story. It was about an orange tree; it had been fertilized and cultivated in abundance so that it might produce early and abundantly in the tree's production. This tree was not to supposed to produce for two more years, but because of all the supplements it got, sure enough it produced early and abundantly. The researchers were very pleased with the results until the following year when a large portion of the tree died and the rest of the tree never produced much after that. True or not, this story is about timing and what God has built into that tree. The tree was designed to produce at a certain time and a certain amount. By tampering with the process, it changed everything.

What causes people to produce above and beyond? When their hearts are rooted and grounded in the good soil of Jesus, and it is a big job to get them there. It takes a lot of effort and time.

Our job is to bring them to a place of development that will produce the fruit of God. This, remember, is maturity, and maturity takes time.

I once rushed some people and ended up losing them because they had no strong fabric in their makeup. Sometimes as young and energetic pastors, we put new people in a servant's position in our churches, and they were not getting the nourishment of God's Word in order to grow. By placing them in this place of responsibility, we cut off their food supply (God's Word), and sure enough, each person got weak and started down the wrong road again, often ending up back in sin and in complete family failure, divorce, and even loss of life.

So what is the answer?

Four Types of People

There are always **four types of people in your church services**. If you don't believe this, then you may have fallen into a trap that says that "the people who come to my services and listen to me preach are all okay with God." With that kind of thinking, you'll do nothing about the protection and future of these people.

Let's see what God says. As we look at 1 Corinthians 14, the subject is tongues, but let's look past that to what is being said about the people in our services. Count them!

> *Therefore tongues are for a sign, not to those who **believe** but to **unbelievers**; but prophesying is not for unbelievers but for those who believe. Therefore if the whole church comes together in one place, and all speak with tongues, and there come in those who are **uninformed** or unbelievers, will they not say that you are out of your mind?*

1 Corinthians 14:22-23

We see three: those who **believe**, those who **don't believe**, and those that are **uninformed**, all in verses twenty-two and twenty-three. And if we take a closer look, we can see that if there are uninformed, then there must be **informed** as well.

These are the four types of people that are in our churches, and all need to be led to green pastures, not to the desert.

Also, there are four types of people that Jesus talks about in Mark four. In Verses 3-8, He tells the parable. In Verses thirteen through twenty, He explains it.

The Wayside Wander

*"The sower sows the word. And these are the ones by the wayside where the word is sown. When they hear, **Satan comes immediately and takes away the word that was sown in their hearts"*** (Mark 4:14-15). We see people who don't know how to protect that which they have received. This is the first type of people who are in our churches. They hear, and they receive it because it is in their heart, and Satan comes immediately. If he doesn't come immediately, then this person has time to place a value on it and protect it. They need a church to help them do that, or at the very least explain what is about to happen so there can be some resistance to Satan coming.

Without knowing what to do next and encouragement to do it right away, these people become easy prey to Satan. The church's responsibility is to warn, encourage, and get them back in the sheepfold, as close to the Shepherd's rod as possible. These are all things that we do to be pleasing to His plan for His people. I believe that when we please Him, He trusts us with more growth. And you know you want growth.

Stony Ground Startup

The second type of person is found in verse sixteen and seventeen:

*These likewise are the ones sown on **stony ground** who, when they hear the word, immediately receive it with gladness; and **they have no root in themselves**, and so endure only for a time. Afterward, when tribulation or persecution arises for the word's sake, immediately they stumble.*

This person received the Word but in the head and not in the heart. See "stony ground." Maybe this is where we get the expression "rock head" or "hard-headed." I don't know, but what I do know is that they are glad to get it, but it doesn't last long because it is not where it needs to be. It is not deep in their heart, or not part of the "makeup" of their lives. It is not what they are going to live their lives by. The Word is good to them, but not part of them. When pressure comes, they fail.

Again, the role of the church here is to help them make the transition from a carnal Christian to a heartfelt, "Word of God" reliant person of God.

The Thorny Burnout

The third person that we see is found in verses eighteen and nineteen:

> Now these are the ones sown **among thorns**; they are the ones who hear the word, and **the cares of this world**, the **deceitfulness of riches**, and **the desires for other things** entering in choke the word, and it becomes unfruitful.

This is a person who places no real value on the Word of God, seeing other things as more important. Eventually, the very thing that should be the most important in their lives becomes nothing. What a shame. If you can keep these people for any length of time, the church's job would be to reestablish godly values.

How valuable is the Word of God in our lives? Without it, life is empty and carries no real purpose. We would end up living out our lives based on the knowledge of the tree of good and evil, void of any real godly existence. How sad, because the ultimate outcome is death.

It's maybe just my opinion, but I think most people that attend American churches fit the description of the first three that Jesus is talking about. That is okay as long as they don't *stay* there. This should be the role of all of our churches—to advance God's people to the become the fourth type of person, as found in Mark 4:20.

The Fruitful Few

Jesus says, "*But these are the ones sown on good ground, those who hear the word, accept it, and bear fruit: some thirtyfold, some sixty, and some a hundred*" (Mark 4:20).

Don't we all want our churches filled with this type of people? Some churches specialize in this one group of people—the first three or four rows of people in our churches, aka the good ground people. But note that the other three types of people need a lot of work before they can produce the fruit that pleases God. And there are a lot of people who fall into those first three types.

> The real work of the church is in the other three types of people.

The "work" that I'm talking about is not in the people who hear and produce, the fruitful people. The real work of the church is in the other three types of people. It takes a lot of work and a lot of creativity in order to reach them, and you are not going to reach them until you keep them around for a while.

How to Keep Them Long Enough

So, as you can see, how we minister to everyone in our churches—from the front rows all the way to the very back—is very important to our God.

To keep them in the church, we try to get them active or involved in doing something. But what they are active in or involved in may be the wrong thing for them and may actually keep them away from the "Word of God," which is the very thing that they need to grow to "good ground."

I love volunteers. At our church, we have between 500-700 per week. Churches need them to help meet the needs of the people. Without them, a church won't be able to keep up with the people. So how important are they? Very. But they can't be a human sacrifice for the betterment of the church to the point they end up failing in their lives. How displeasing this must be to the God, who goes after the one lost sheep!

So we have very strict rules that apply to all. When you volunteer, you must also be in church services, sitting and listing to the Word of God. It is more important that they grow to maturity by hearing and applying the Word of God than all of the volunteer time put together. If we don't stay after this, the people will think that their volunteer time was their church time, and they will end up a derelict. That's why people who worked for years in a volunteer position no longer attend our church or any other. We lost them because our need was above God's plan for their life. God forgive me!

God was not pleased with my management of His people. And "not pleased" means no growth to my church. Why should He send people into the church when the people are going to be used up and spiritually abused for the ministry's sake? I couldn't govern this as I preached, so I had to remind the ministries leaders to make sure their volunteers were in church also. I found that if you can schedule them to volunteer, you should also schedule them for that church service.

Some of the department leaders did a good job watching over their volunteers, but most need to be encouraged on a regular basis. We need to check up on our department leaders and the volunteers to make sure they get the Word of God to live by. Most people will accept our rules and get on board if they truly understand why we insist they get in service to hear the Word of God. We just explain to them the importance of why we do what we do and how important it is to hear the Word of God under the anointing of their pastor, not some TV preacher or live stream or download. The anointing for their lives is found being in church in person. When people understand, they seem to feel better about getting into church.

Stir Them Up

Hebrews 10:24 tells us, *"And let us consider one another in order to stir up love and good works."*

It seems to me that most people don't know what they need until you tell them and show them. If they did, then they wouldn't need pastors and church leaders. That is exactly what "good" shepherds do in caring for God's people.

I don't know why, but when we start to please God, then our churches start to grow. We are so foolish at times. When our churches start to grow, something happens in the heart and mind of some of us shepherds—we all start to think that it was *us* who caused the growth.

One of the things that I see is that we forget what we were doing when the church started to grow. It would be like God saying, "Good job," and then we stop doing what it is that got the compliment. Stay focused on the work that God has set before you.

Followers of God, let's work at staying there. And let's work at getting all the people to become front row people. **Expand your rows.**

Chapter 17

Truth about Your Labor

In a conversation I had with a friend and fellow pastor, I asked how his church was doing, and he responded, "Good, thanks." I wanted to know what he considered "good," so I continued to ask questions about the activity of his church. I asked a question, and his response shocked me, and to this day I have not been able to get it out of my thinking. I asked him how many church services they had each week. He said that they had one service, just Sunday morning. I was surprised by the answer, so I asked "Just one? Is that good for the people?"

He answered, "I don't know, but it is good for me." I realized that I needed to let it go and just shut up if I was to remain any kind of a friend; that is hard for a mouthy person like me.

Early in our ministry, I found that the more opportunities people have to come to church, the more they will come. (You should read that again.)

> Early in our ministry, I found that the more opportunities people have to come to church, the more they will come.

More services bring more work, more work brings more opportunity, and more opportunity brings greater maturity—not to mention more money to pay your bills.

Church Is More than Sunday Mornings

In today's society, people can't always come to church on Sunday mornings; they work, or it might be that it is the only day that they can spend with the family. So we started to have more church services to meet the needs of the people.

At first, it was a total failure; very few came, and it seemed a big waste of time. But I couldn't stop because I had to do what God wanted me to do, so I stayed with it and learned how to make the other services during the week as wonderful as our Sunday morning.

That is when God first spoke to me that **what I treat as common will always remain common, but whatever I treat as special will become special.** I was treating our extra services as very common. A small service warranted a small effort on my part. And if the staff is small-thinking, well, then they will always treat this extra service as second-class. Our children's church for Sunday morning was great, but the extra services were just a babysitting effort only. God wanted me to bring the extra services up to Sunday morning quality—in every way, as good as a Sunday morning. Everything had to change, and everything did.

So the new policy was to make it different and as good as it could be with nothing left out. It was the same with the youth services as well as music department and everything else. Hard work? You bet. In time, it all started to pay off in every way—souls, maturity, growth, and even financially.

The people who wanted to worship in a midweek service just came out. Many went to another church on Sunday, but their church had only one service, and they found themselves at one of our midweek services. We didn't plan on taking anyone from other churches or try to get them to come to our church, but it just happened.

I have to be honest and say that it was very hard work for everyone. It is not easy to get people to come in and volunteer at church at night when they have worked hard all day. Many didn't even get dinner. But when it was explained, they responded.

At first, I would see more people on the platform leading worship than in the audience, but it didn't take long for God to be pleased, and He started to add to the church service. About 50-60% of the people at our mid-week service just couldn't come on a Sunday. Our mid-week service is our second-largest service of the week, our Sunday night service is the third-largest, our Saturday morning is the fourth-largest, and our Thursday morning is the fifth, and our Friday night is the sixth—not to mention our Spanish-language service and the multiple repeat services.

At one time, we had eleven services in a single week—all-out services. Lots of work. Lots of people. Lots of fun. Lots of rewards!

Dealing with the staff was an interesting experience; not all wanted to work that hard. If I left it up to them, they would have said "no" to all the hard work that is required over and above their regular hours. I couldn't let the staff dictate to me the direction of the church; only God could tell me what He wanted. After all, it is His church, and we are in the following business.

We try never to take advantage of any of God's people, even the ones that work for the ministry. If they worked hard and put in extra time, then we would give them comp-days to make up for all their extra work. We couldn't give them money because we didn't have that kind of extra money. The staff loves those extra days off with pay. Remember, your staff cannot become a human sacrifice for the ministry. That would get us in trouble with God.

All of us are people who want church growth. Why, if you can't get your staff to work hard for people and for the maturity of God's people and for church growth, then you have the wrong people on your staff.

One time a minister sent me his resume wanting a position with our church. When I read the resume, I was very impressed; he had all the tools and the experience anyone could desire. I called him, and we talked. I wasn't going to hire him, but I cared enough about him to tell him about what was important to a senior pastor besides all of his ability.

I told him that what I look for is not just experience or abilities but if that person has a desire for church growth. I told him to restructure his resume and add a section in it about how he wanted to take his experience and abilities to support the vision of the senior pastor for church growth; that is what pastors want.

He did what I suggested, and he re-sent them to other churches and got a lot of great responses and was hired immediately by a big church. He is very happy to this day.

Your staff should be on board with "hard work," or it won't be long before God replaces them.

Time to Move On

In Daniel chapter five, we see a new king by the name of Belshazzar, a down-the-line relative of King Nebuchadnezzar. He thinks that he has it made in his impregnable city, so he decides to have an all-out drunken party. During the party, a hand comes out of heaven and writes on the wall of one of the rooms (you know the story). It shocks all the people, but they cannot read it, so they call the old man Daniel to interpret it. And he does.

> "And this is the inscription that was written: MENE, MENE, TEKEL, UPHARSIN. This is the interpretation of each word. MENE: God has numbered your kingdom, and finished it; TEKEL: **You have been weighed in the balances, and found wanting**; PERES: Your kingdom has been divided, and given to the Medes and Persians."

Daniel 5:25-28

Many times God will check us out to see if we fit into His plan. And when we don't, He moves us on to a place that is better for us and His plan. If He checked out this corrupt king, then He for sure will check out the hearts of His people to see if they fit into His plan.

Many times I would find myself with people on staff who I thought did not fit the hard work plan that God had given to our church. Somehow, God would place them on my heart, and I just knew that God would be moving them on. Sometimes I would have to wait a year or more, but it always came to pass. I would always make sure that they knew it was their call, so I would even give them some time to make sure. But it always turned out the same, and they felt they just had to leave.

Please don't misunderstand—they were not bad. They are wonderful; they just were not going to fit where God was going to take us. So in His love for them and us, He moves them on.

Sometimes we forget the benefits of hard work for God's people, and just being there for people, His love. Lots of people got saved, people were healed, families were restored, marriages were mended—and still are to this day. All from exhausting *hard work.*

No wonder I could say that I could feel God's pleasure. That always translates to church growth.

> Hard work is not what you feel like doing but what God plans for you to do. Exhaustion is not a bad feeling, but it becomes a badge of pleasure that you wear.

As you know, the Bible says, "*Whatever you sow, you reap.*" We were sowing God's goodness in the people, and we started to reap His blessings.

Hard work is not what you feel like doing but what God plans for you to do. Exhaustion is not a bad feeling, but it becomes a badge of pleasure that you wear.

We just know God was in it and that satisfied our souls. Exhausted? Yes, but it was a good exhaustion.

What Can You Do For People

By the way, we didn't start those other services to get more money, but boy, it came in. And to this day, those services more than pay their way. The extra money in a city like ours makes all the difference in the world, and I believe that God knew that when He inspired us to work hard.

Not only did the money start to come in, but so did the people. Many people started to make our church their home because they worked on Sunday and could only come on another time, and we were the only church in town that had those other services for them. The more they came, the more committed they became. They started to bring their friends and families.

I remember a woman who got saved on a Wednesday night, went home, and brought fourteen of her family members that following Sunday! She couldn't come on future Sundays because she worked, so for this one week she took the day off just to bring her family. By the way, they all got saved—all fourteen of them—and now they come on Sundays, and some even come on Wednesdays with her. How fun is that? Thank God, yes! But also God rewarded the hard work.

We just wanted to meet the needs of God's people. That is the attitude we had and the attitude of our church. **It's about what we can do for people, not what they can do for us.**

One time we found out that there were a lot of people who had disabled children and could not go to church because they had to watch them. If they went to church, they would be asked to leave because they couldn't handle the children. The churches were not being rude; they were just not equipped to minister to these children and their families. So they just didn't go to church at all.

What would God have us to do? We were not equipped ourselves. But God spoke to me to get equipped and have a special class for them. It had to include one-on-one volunteers at times, but the people rose up to the opportunity, and the families came and they told their friends. To this day, it is one of the most blessed spots in our church.

The Presence of Momentum

One of the great benefits of multiple services is the momentum and excitement of the church. When people take on a church as their own, something wonderful takes place, an excitement that brings momentum. It's a God thing, a "good" thing. When the people come to church and they know that the church is a lot more than a service, excited people bring the church into an exciting encounter with God. This encounter causes the people to experience the momentum of God. So when they come, they get touched by Him and directed by Him, and they never leave the same. **His presence generates momentum, His presence brings His encounter, and His encounter changes lives forever.**

> His presence generates momentum, His presence brings His encounter, and His encounter changes lives forever.

This all started with the right attitude towards our labors. Hard work is good before God, and there will be a payoff, and it is **His presence.**

So many pastors give up on multiple services. And I admit it is easy to do. The excuses are always the same: no one shows up, we can't afford to do that, our city is different than others, our people are not used to going to church two times per week, it would just wear the servers and staff out. This gives us a lot of justification for why we should not do it.

Put spiritually, "the mountain" is just too big. That's true, and it always will be—except for those who don't put their eyes on the mountain but keep their eyes on the God who can reap where He did not sow, a God that can do whatever He wants. That equals church growth.

The real deciding factor should be, "Is it pleasing to God for His people to get more of God or not?" If you think not, then don't even try to have multiple services or "encounters." It won't work.

I found that if it is pleasing to God, then it is His will. And no more needs to be said.

Galatians 6:7 says, *"Do not be deceived, God is not mocked; for whatever a man sows, that he will also reap."* It goes on to say, *"For he who sows to his flesh will of the flesh reap corruption, but he who sows to the Spirit will of the Spirit reap everlasting life. And let us not grow weary while doing good, for in due season we shall reap if we do not lose heart"* (vs 8-9).

James 2:18 reminds us, *"But someone will say, 'You have faith, and I have works.' Show me your faith without your works, and I will show you my faith by my works."*

May I give you a little hint on how to get your services to grow? The people pay attention to whatever you talk about from the pulpit. You are anointed by God to talk about His Word, and the people will listen. Use that anointing that comes from the pulpit to talk up whatever it is that God wants the people to get involved in. If you know He wants them to come to your midweek service, then talk it up from the pulpit—why they should come, the benefits of coming, when to come, and what to expect. Most will not come, but those who do will be blessed, and that will bring God's pleasure.

Chapter 18

Me

The Bible says, numerous times, that we should examine ourselves from time to time to make sure we are okay with God. The big problem with being a pastor is dealing with the flesh. It a problem for everyone, but I think pastors should take this chapter very seriously.

The church was growing and growing; it seemed like whatever we did, God would just bless us and continue to bless us. Wow, life was good! I truly have to say that there were not many times like this one. In one brief period of time, we had over 600 people join the church in thirty days; there was a waiting line to take the church membership class. I had never experienced anything like it before or since.

> Jesus can get an "honorable mention" in the midst of our attempt to boast about ourselves.

As a pastor, I was on top of the world. And that was the problem, in a nutshell—I was on top of the "world," instead of being in Jesus. I wanted people to see and recognize what was going on so much that I started to brag. Not like you might think, but it was bragging any way you look at it. Most of us pastors have learned to brag about what God is doing with "undercover expressions." In other words, we will brag and cover up our bragging by mentioning Jesus. **Jesus can get an "honorable mention" in the midst of our attempt to boast about ourselves.**

Therefore, to us it really didn't seem to be what we might call bragging. But the truth is, you can't fool Jesus because He reads the heart. In my attempt to cover my bragging, I said to the congregation one Sunday morning, "This church is growing so fast that you have to get into line to just become a member. We should get a take-a-number machine in order to become a member." That doesn't sound so bad, but what I was really saying was, "Aren't we wonderful? And look how great a pastor I am. People are crowding into this place, and that proves I'm a great pastor."

You know, as well as I do, that it is Jesus that is doing the work, not us. We are privileged to be an instrument of His love towards His people. Wow, how amazing of a God do we serve that constantly operates in mercy in the face of our folly!

Glory Only in the Lord

Paul writes, *"that no flesh should glory in His presence... that, as it is written, "He who glories, let him glory in the LORD"* 1 Corinthians 1:29,31).

Our God is so serious about this subject. The word glory and its meaning are described in the book of Exodus where we find Moses talking to God. *"And he said, 'Please, show me Your glory.' Then He said, 'I will make all My goodness pass before you, and I will proclaim the name of the LORD before you. I will be gracious to whom I will be gracious, and I will have compassion on whom I will have compassion'"* (Exodus 33:18-19).

Then a few verses later we read, *"So it shall be, while **My glory passes by**, that I will put you in the cleft of the rock, and will cover you with My hand while I pass by"* (**Exodus 33:22**).

"Glory" is God's manifested goodness. When I glorify God, I'm proclaiming the goodness of God, and when I see His goodness at work—that is His glory. The manifested goodness of God being expressed is far from what I was doing when I was "undercover bragging," and God knew it.

What happened next is what will always happen—**God will not be in something that is not of Him.** He stopped bringing people in, and that short time of great church growth ended. Why? Because He truly loves me, and the path that I was on could only end up in a major failure. If He had let me get away with this foolish behavior, I would have thought that I was "right" with God and would have kept on doing "wrong" in the glorying of myself.

It was a shock that shook me to my very core, and you would have thought that I would have learned my lesson, but I didn't.

Sometimes we pastors are not as smart as we think we are (or hope people think we are). We see the depth of God in His Word and even teach it, but think often to ourselves that the Word somehow is for others and not for our lives. We are anointed to preach and teach the Word of God, but **we are not any more anointed to keep the Word than anyone else.**

Maybe we think like that because we teach His Word and we know it. We, at times, don't take the Word of God as if it is written personally to us, the good and the bad and all the warnings. Even though I'm a pastor, the love of the world is still operating in me at times. I'm reminded of 1 John 2:16, which says, *"For all that is in the world—**the lust of the flesh, the lust of the eyes, and the pride of life**—is not of the Father but is of the world."*

That was me. I didn't like it, but it was me. Often times this old relationship with the world's ways pops up in us and works against God's plan for our future. It stops all that He has for us, and all the blessing that we so dearly desire. We don't even recognize it, because we are so familiar with living in the world system that it is just comfortable to us, normal, and often times acceptable. We don't think that it is contrary to the ways and the will of God. Remember, we get this thinking from the tree of knowledge of good and evil.

Keep in mind that the first thing that Adam and Eve did after they received the knowledge of good and evil from the tree was to feel insecure (uncovered). So they did something to comfort themselves—they tried to cover themselves (Gen. 3:7). I tried to cover myself in my insecurities by bragging.

This kind of insecurity plays a big role in how we do life and how we pastor our churches. Insecurity will cause us to make bad decisions in our lives and ministries, and that is what happened when I try to be something that I'm not.

Determine the Destiny of Your Future

We fight battles on so many fronts. I don't know which one is yours, but I do know some of mine, so maybe you can relate to some of my battlegrounds.

The mind can tell me what to think about and what I think about myself. My mind could tell me that I'm good or no good, unimportant or very important, nice or unkind, stupid or over-confident, too lazy or too aggressive—the list can go on and on. But what if I could share a truth that can settle it all at one time, no matter what the issues are with which we battle? A principle or a truth that is so simple that it is often times overlooked. This little truth has set me free and can save you years of unprofitable battles.

I found that how people see themselves will determine the destiny of their future. If I think I can, then I most likely will. But if I don't think I can, then I most likely won't even try, so I won't put in a full effort because I'm expecting negative results. But if I bring Jesus into my mental calculations, then that which might seem impossible now becomes very possible.

> How people see themselves will determine the destiny of their future.

Matthew 19:26 says, *"But Jesus looked at them and said to them, "With men this is impossible, but with God all things are possible."*

We just sometimes forget and need to be reminded, and we need to get our minds in the right place.

What a job God has, to try and train us in the midst of the battles of life and still keep His church healthy! If we could just get our minds on Him and off ourselves, it would truly change the world that we live in.

Keep Your Eyes on Jesus

What if I could show you how this works so that you can fulfill all that God has for you? Sound good? I'll show you from the Word of God, so you don't think that it is just some crazy old man's idea.

First, let us establish what the makeup of man looks like. Paul writes to the church at Thessalonica, *"Now may the God of peace Himself sanctify you **completely**; and may your **whole spirit, soul, and body*** *be preserved blameless at the coming of our Lord Jesus Christ"* (1 Thessalonians 5:23).

We see the **whole of person** being sanctified completely or set apart for the coming of the Lord. We, therefore, are made up of three parts: body, soul, and spirit. Let me lay them out like this:

SOUL

BODY   SPIRIT

(Diagram #1)

Let's now talk about the function of these parts (our makeup).

"The soul" is the working of the mind, thinking, passions, will, desires, and emotions. It all flows out of the mind or soul.

SOUL
**mind • passions
will • desires
emotions
thinking**

(Diagram #2)

"The body" is the working of fleshly feelings, desires, lusts, cravings, carnality, and all that is supported by our feelings.

BODY
**worldliness
carnality
lusts • cravings
fleshly feelings**

(Diagram #3)

"The spirit" is the real heart of man that adapts to the leading by the Holy Spirit. Some may call this our spirit working together with the Holy Spirit.

SPIRIT
**Spirit of God
and
spirit of man
(inside)**

(Diagram #4)

Galatians 5:16-17 tells us, "*I say then: Walk in the Spirit, and you shall not fulfill the lust of the flesh. For the flesh lusts against the Spirit, and the Spirit against the flesh; and these are contrary to one another, so that you do not do the things that you wish.*"

To walk in the Spirit is to live out life by operating in spiritual ways or by the Word of God. If you do, you will not fulfill the lust of the body or flesh. For the flesh (body) and the Spirit "lust" against each other. The Bible says they are contrary to one another and that the spirit stops you from doing the fleshly things you would like to do. (Note: It doesn't say anything about soul.)

(Diagram #5)

The soul of man, his mind or his thinking, now becomes the battle-ground for your future. Whichever way the soul follows—the flesh or the Spirit—it will overpower the other remaining part, and the soul becomes **the pivot** to the future of success or of failure.

The Spirit and the flesh can't work together; they are at odds with each other. If the "flesh" (body) cannot work with the "spirit," then the flesh will want to work with the soul or the thinking of man. It is the same with the spirit; it also cannot work with the flesh, or body, so the spirit will also want to work with the soul. Again, any two that work together void out the power of the third.

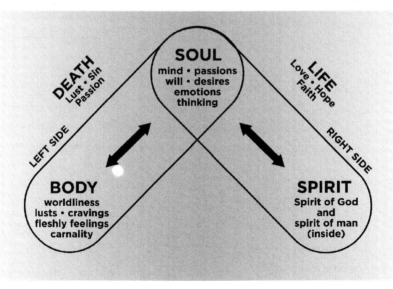

(Diagram #6)

Example: if the spirit works with the soul, it voids out the power of the flesh/body, or if the flesh body works with the soul/mind than it voids out the power of the spirit. This stops us from ever "walking after the Spirit" or living out our life according to the Word of God. At this juncture, we are helpless and hopeless and now have become slaves to the flesh.

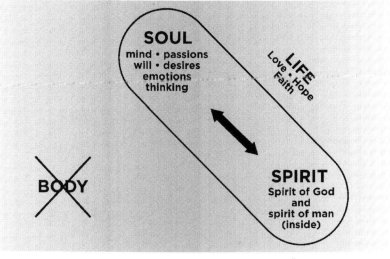

(Diagram #7)

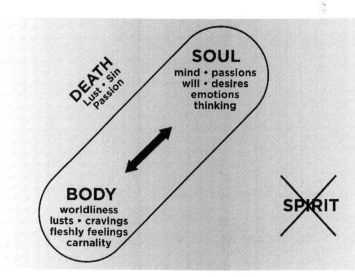

(Diagram #8)

Paul writes, "**Knowing** this, that our old man was crucified with Him, that the body of sin might be done away with, **that we should no longer be slaves of sin**" (Romans 6:6).

He goes on to explain it this way:

> **Therefore do not let sin reign in your mortal body, that you should obey it in its lusts.** And do not present your members as instruments of unrighteousness to sin, but present yourselves to God as being alive from the dead, and your members as instruments of righteousness to God. For sin shall not have dominion over you, for you are not under law but under grace.
>
> What then? Shall we sin because we are not under law but under grace? Certainly not! **Do you not know that to whom you present yourselves slaves to obey, you are that one's slaves whom you obey, whether of sin leading to death, or of obedience leading to righteousness?** But God be thanked that though you were slaves of sin, yet you **obeyed from the heart** [soul and spirit working together] that form of doctrine to which you were delivered.
>
> (Romans 6:12-17 brackets are my injection)

Romans 8:5-8 tells us,

> For those **who live according to the flesh set their minds on the things of the flesh,** but those who **live according to the Spirit, the things of the Spirit. For to be carnally minded is death, but to be spiritually minded is life and peace.** Because the carnal mind is enmity against God; for it is not

*subject to the law of God, nor indeed can be. So then, **those who are in the flesh cannot please God.***

This really boils down to our call. We get in trouble when we live in the natural, not realizing that it is contrary to the ways of the spirit, and we fail at what we are trying to do. Living in the "right" side produces life; living in the "left" side brings about death (or failure to our churches). The "left side thinking" comes from the Garden, the tree of the knowledge of good and evil. But the "right side thinking" comes from the cross of Calvary—grace and faith.

It's Not About Numbers

Some years back, I received a free copy of a magazine whose cover had the heading of "The Top 100 Churches in America." Wow, I thought to myself, this should be interesting. The magazine was very well organized and broke down this evaluation by states. Also, the size was determined by the number of people that attended the weekend services.

After reading all the interesting stats, I began doing the math and asked the staff who track the number of people at our church how many people were coming on any given weekend. The numbers came in and I compared them to the reports in the magazine. Much to my surprise, we turned out to be the second-largest church in California and the eighteenth largest church in America. I was shocked and felt a new feeling, a sense of accomplishment. This was a really good feeling, and it started me down a road I wish I had never gone down.

From that sense of accomplishment came a desire to present our church to the world, for we have never been recognized for anything good. Keep in mind what I mean about "good." I always felt like we were a second-class church, and everybody else always felt better than us. But now it was our time to show off a little...

When the bragging starts, God stops. I told the congregation that we were the second-largest church in California, and the way we were growing would soon become the first. After all, we were many years younger than the number one church, and we were very different from almost any other church. The world needed to know how special this church was, and there needed to be someone to shout out its praise.

You might be wondering, "Did I bring Jesus into this shout out?" You bet I did. The typical "undercover bragging" that we all do at times, well it was in full force with me. We say that "Jesus is doing something at our church," and He was. That is not bad but the right thing to say. But when that is just to cover up your real meaning –"Look how great our church is; acknowledge and recognize us for what we are doing"—it is bragging, and you will get in trouble with God.

Where is the spirit, and where is the flesh? Can you see the operation of the flesh and the soul?

I had our administrator contact the magazine for the information needed about the church for the next couple of years, and it was printed each year. We had arrived.

While all this was happening, something that was on the inside of me was changing. The change felt good, and it would have been hard for me to believe that what I was doing was *wrong* in the sight of God. It felt too good to be wrong. Could this be a feeling from the Garden? I think so!

The change that took place was on multiple levels. First, I started to feel good about myself—not in a healthy way as one might think. What I felt was a natural good not a spiritual "good."

The difference is that the natural appeals to the senses, where pride becomes its fruit. But the spiritual "good" appeals to the heart, and the fruit of that is humility.

Exaltation does not bring humility, but humility brings exaltation.

I was out of control, and pride had its grip on me. I had gone completely "left side." The flesh and the soul were busy doing what felt good to the flesh, and they work well together to destroy our futures.

Any time that God senses "pride," He starts to back off. Remember James 4:6: *"But He gives more grace. Therefore He says: 'God resists the proud, But gives grace to the humble.'"*

> The difference is that the natural appeals to the senses, where pride becomes its fruit. But the spiritual "good" appeals to the heart, and the fruit of that is humility.

I am sure because of love, He didn't want to, but He had to. The church started to lose many great people—about 8,000—and I was *stunned.* He got my attention. The hard way!

They Are Not There For You

The next level of change was my relationship with the people. They had become an important *number* to me instead of the "love of His life" in my care. The care that I gave them in the past was now second to my self-exaltation.

When you have 24,000 people in church, it takes a while for you to start noticing that you are going down in size. So no changes were made on the inside of me until I noticed something was wrong. We were hemorrhaging people, and I didn't know why. I looked at all the different department leaders to make sure they were doing their jobs, and I found that they were doing their jobs better than me!

I started to believe that our staff didn't see the importance of church growth, and I put pressure on them for more church growth, as if they could make the difference. But in truth, the church growth that you and I want is the growth that comes not just from our staff, but from God's presence. His presence comes when the spirit and the soul work together—the "right side." This is contrary to the feeling that operates when the flesh and soul work together.

Finally, my wife said something—kind, but blunt—that got my attention about numbering His people. She said it was as if they didn't have much importance and had become just a number to satisfy my ego and insecurities. Of course, my "undercover bragging" didn't help.

God backed off big time, because He had to. After all, He is God. It was as if my spirit and soul forgot how to work together. Now it was my time to repent and ask God to forgive me. And I quickly did.

By this time, I was in my seventies, and it was time for me to get out of the way for the next generation to come on and be all that it could be. As soon as I got out of the way, God started to grow His church again. Now, I'm there to help these young church leaders avoid making the same stupid mistakes I've made, to stay on the "right side."

I think they are listening; are you?

Pride Is Contagious

The third level of change brings on something that I never saw before—my pride was a contagious disease, and the people around me had caught it. And the only cure was for me to repent and acknowledge my sins before my staff. Nothing could be worse than this for a pastor because we want those who work for us to admire us and not see us as spiritual buffoons.

Much to my surprise, my transparency became a refreshing thing, as transparency always does, and the staff thought more of me than before. **Transparency always leads to humility, which will transport you to dependency, which is true spirituality** (hope you got that).

Pride (independent, selfish desire) is so subtle. It comes in and feels so good to the natural side of our make-up. How could something like this be wrong? It takes us immediately out of the care of God and dependency on God that we need.

> Transparency always leads to humility, which will transport you to dependency, which is true spirituality.

It acts like nightshade. It is poisonous on one hand, but there are several kinds of nightshade that have been used as herbal medicines. To the world, pride can be a medicine; it can help people to get to where they think they need to be. This is worldly success. But to the church (God's people), pride is a vicious poison that will kill your life and your future and the future of those that associate with you.

We must remain dependent on God, for it is in that dependency that we gather His strength. It may be hard to imagine, but the most spiritual person is just the person who is the most dependent on God.

Moses is described as the meekest of all men, and look how these two different translations address the same verse: "(*Now the man Moses was **very meek**, above all the men which were upon the face of the earth.*)" (Numbers 12:3 KJV) "(*Now the man Moses was **very humble**, more than all men who were on the face of the earth.*)" (Numbers 12:3)

Moses was very dependent on God, and that is why God could use him. It is the same today.

Remember Hebrew 11:34. Seven of some of the most powerful words in the Bible are *"out of weakness were made strong."*

Two Sides of God's Success

In order to be successful, two very important things must be acknowledged. It is almost like a two-sided coin.

The first side of the coin is the great position that Jesus has paid for that has made you and me a new creature in Christ Jesus. You must know who you are *in Christ Jesus*. We are the righteousness of God in Christ Jesus, we are more than conquers in Christ Jesus, we can do all things through Christ Jesus, and so on. It is a very important position to recognize. But your position can come with pride. The position must be a platform for operation and not a platform for self-confidence or self-accomplishments.

The position of "being in Christ Jesus" opens the door for God to be with us in our endeavors of life, and gives us access to His power on our behalf. When we think that because I'm a child of God, therefore I can do all things, we sometimes forget that part that screams out **dependency** "through Christ Jesus."

The other side of the coin is this big word "dependency"—recognition that nothing of any godly importance is going to get done without Him. I'm just not smart enough, gifted enough, or even talented enough to make it work the way He wants it to work.

I don't even think faith works without dependency. The entire eleventh chapter of Hebrews talks about men and women of God who did great things—so great that He devotes the entire chapter to these amazing people. But He finishes the chapter with the insight that they were all very dependent on God, and their dependence made them very strong.

Here is a thought: "deep love becomes dependent love" or deep love incorporates others. I'm deeply in love with my wife, and I'm very dependent on her to fulfill our relationship as husband and wife. Without her doing her part and me doing my part, the relationship wouldn't work so well. Wouldn't it be the same with Jesus and His bride?

Dependency becomes the act of deep love and respect, *"For in Christ Jesus neither circumcision nor uncircumcision avails anything, but faith working through love"* (Galatians 5:6).

The verse says that it is not human effort or human acts but by faith that is so dependent that you won't want the results without Him being involved in it. This is "love." God is looking for the most dependent people to operate in His church. I think He calls them lovers.

How dependent are we when it comes to this ministry that God has asked us to do? That, my friends, will determine the level of God's power released on our behalf.

Are our souls lined up with His Spirit, or are our souls listening to our flesh? For me, it has got to be my soul and my spirit working together for His glory—manifested goodness.

Chapter 19:

The Power of Transparency

As a young man, I overheard a very seasoned preacher say, "I have to be the smartest person in my church." The words just stuck with me all my life. I remember that when I heard him say those words, I knew it was wrong, and there was no way I could ever live up to that statement. Maybe for that old preacher it was true, and when I think about it, the statement could have been true because he only had about twenty-five people in his church. How he saw himself was his business, but how I saw myself had to be important to me, and I wanted to see myself how God wanted me to see myself.

The heart is the ears of the soul, and in my heart I honestly saw myself as a person who did not know much about what I was doing. For me to present myself to a congregation as the smartest person in the room would have just been a big lie. Can you imagine trying to pretend to be something you're not every time you get up before your congregation? Now that would be real bondage—bondage in the time when you need to be free to be what God would have you to be. Embracing that is being a person of integrity.

When we try to be something that we are not, we are fooling ourselves and stopping God from using us as He desires. Find your place—your own place—and enjoy it. If the people around you do not like it, too bad. **You are what God made you to be, and God knew it from the beginning of your life. He is not shocked by it.**

> You are what God made you to be, and God knew it from the beginning of your life. He is not shocked by it.

Jeremiah 13:23 says, *"Can the Ethiopian change his skin or the leopard its spots? Then may you also do good who are accustomed to do evil."*

The Holy Spirit Is the Real Teacher

Maybe we are not as extreme as the old preacher who had to be smarter than everyone else, but most of us have areas of our personal makeup that are something we don't want others to see. Maybe we just feel insecure about ourselves in general, and we feel unqualified to fit the title of our office. So we present ourselves different than we really are. Is that not manipulation? In truth, God cannot be part of that, so He gives us lots of time to change.

For years, I beat myself up over the way I looked and the way I sounded. I tried so hard to change to become what I thought a minister should look like and sound like. I'm sure my wife even wanted me to change at times, but in her kindness she would tell me all was great and a leopard can't change his spots. She was giving me the peace I needed to continue.

We don't realize the power of ministry. Many times people would come up to me and tell me how much they got out of the message. They would say something like, "My life will never be the same." Meanwhile, I was thinking to myself, "That was a horrible message!"

Many times over the years, people would come up to me and ask if I remembered when I said some particular thing. Thinking about what they said, I was sure that I would never say what it was they heard, but somehow they heard it. Where did it come from? There was no mistake on their part as to what they heard. I was always confused by what they said until I realized it was not me who said it, but it was *God* who spoke to them. In each case, the words that they heard brought real meaningful blessings to their lives. God spoke through me to them. But not like you would think.

So many times we present ourselves as the teachers of the church. And rightfully so; in a way, you could say that we do teach. But truth be known, the only real teacher of the church is the Holy Spirit. As we communicate God's Word, it is the Holy Spirit who speaks into the people's hearts.

Many times, I would be communicating the Word of Truth, but it is only when the Holy Spirit takes that truth and speaks into the heart of the person that truth becomes alive in them and has the power to change their lives.

Transparency helps people to identify with you so that when God speaks to them it may become easier for them to hear. **Real transparency enhances the ability of the Spirit to touch the lives of the people.**

> Real transparency enhances the ability of the Spirit to touch the lives of the people.

Many times I would start a church service off by saying, "If you have come to hear what a man has to say, you have made your first mistake. It is not about what a man says, but what God has to say, so you should train yourself to go to church expecting God to speak to you, for the Holy Spirit is the real teacher." Sometimes I would say, "I'm just the dumbest man of all. God uses me to show how great and smart He is."

This comment can be shocking to a lot of people and unacceptable to others, but will build a true confidence in the one they should be confident in. The Holy Spirit is the true teacher of the church.

Looking back at some of the things that I feel that God used to build a large church, transparency is one of the key elements. This puts the weight of the church back on the One who is the true Head of the Church, not on my abilities or yours. It is not about you or me, except in a very small way. It is not about my looks or my education, talent or gifting. A church should be built on God as the Head and not a man.

Only transparency puts God back on in His rightful position. It is hard on our egos—I understand that—but it is the right way to build a healthy church. Let God speak in His church.

Interpreter

Years ago, I heard this man who had a very large church on the other side of the world. Sometimes he would have guest speakers in from America; he interpreted for some of them so that the words that his congregation could understand the words his guest spoke. He did that because he really loved his people and wanted the best for them. It was not that the people preaching were saying wrong things, but their words would not have been received with a depth of understanding because of the difference in language and culture. So what the people heard was not exactly how it was said, but the words were received with the proper cultural understanding.

Has anyone ever thought that God could do the same thing with the people He loves? Somehow the things that you said were being heard differently then you may have said them.

Now, I don't believe that if what you say is "off the wall" that He will put you back "on the wall." But if what you say is His truth, then He will see that His truth will resonate within His people.

God is always the teacher. So just be you. God loves you and backs you.

Be Yourself, Transparently

I remember one preacher who so admired another minister that he copied every move and even took on his southern accent. It was funny, because when he opened his mouth, if you didn't know better, you would have sworn he was from the Deep South. I happened to know that the guy was from the south—born and raised in southern *California*, where there is no southern accent.

Even though the other preachers have had great success in his ministry, nowhere does God want us to follow men and their styles. In fact, Paul writes, "Therefore **be imitators of God as dear children**" (Ephesians 5:1).

A man who imitates other men is destined for failure. Yes, the man from Southern California failed, and how sad that is. If we truly trust God, should we not truly trust God and be transparent in every area of our lives? Every area means *every area*. What is there to hide? Because everything that you are exposed in is an area you're free in.

I'm **not** talking about exposing personal intimacy functions. No one cares about that part of your life. But the light could and should shine on some of the personal failures that you have gone through and how you have overcome them in the power of Jesus. This in itself gives great hope to the people in your church, because if God can use us with the problem areas of our lives, then God can use them also.

This kind of transparency builds attainable goals for the people to be able to overcome as their pastor did. It also shows that you are anointed—anointed to preach and teach His Word but also that are no more anointed to *keep* His Word than anyone else. You must put the Word to work like everyone else. Transparency builds true confidence in God and not in a man, which is the exact opposite of what a lot of pastors might think.

We Learn From Mistakes

As a young minister, I had a hard time with this because I was married three times before I married Deborah. As I mentioned earlier, I married one woman two times, and she ran off with someone else. And then I married another woman, and it only lasted fifty-eight days before she threw me out. The truth is that I never left anyone; they dumped me and went off with other people.

This was one of the hardest times of my life. I was completely broken and started realizing that the only hope for my existence would be found in Christ. I wasn't thinking about my future at that point of my life; I was fighting for my very existence.

I went to church for help but only found hypocrisy. After I told my story, they threw me out of the church and said that anyone who had been divorced three times had to be wrong, they didn't want a person like me in their church, and told me never to come back.

I was devastated to my core. Maybe they were right; maybe there was something dreadfully wrong with me. All I knew is that I no longer wanted to live. Life was one big failure.

In those days, one divorce was bad enough, and it was treated as if that person had committed an unpardonable sin. In some churches, the people were allowed to stay in church but were not allowed to do any work in or for the church. They were not allowed even to drive a bus or clean a room.

For me it was a different story—I wasn't even allowed to go to church! I wonder what Jesus is going to say about that kind of thinking. After all, He is the same one who said, **"He who is without sin among you, let him throw a stone at her first"** (John 8:7).

I found a church that would accept me and love me for who or what I was. The pastor loved me and welcomed me. There, my faith was allowed to grow, and my love started to become deep.

Who was right or who was wrong in my divorces was no longer the issue. After all, I was in my early twenties. But soon I was in my mid-thirties and married again to God's most wonderful girl, my Deby. These last forty years with her has been the very best part of my life.

We were confronted with how to deal with our pasts—would we cover it up or use it as a lesson that lots of people could relate to? Would we hide or use it to build hope for those people who have lost their hope because of the tragedy of personal failures? For us, we took a very bad past and became very transparent about it. Instead of people getting upset and leaving the church, it worked in the very opposite. It helped, and transparency once again set the people (and us) **free**.

A lot of people are just too egotistical to be transparent or to take correction from anyone.

> Let's all stop trying to be something we are not and let Him be what He is—God.

God leaves this as a choice of each person, but I truly believe that it will hinder what God has for you if you don't choose transparency. **Scary true but edifying to all.**

Let's all stop trying to be something we are not and let Him be what He is—God.

Chapter 20

The Value of a Goat

"What are you talking about? Goats? In my church? Not a chance! They could not stay; they would feel too strange and would have to leave. My church is only for sheep," one pastor proclaimed. "I hate goats; they just go about butting this and butting that. Give me the sheep."

"I am a sheepherder, not a goat farmer," another pastor said. But the truth is that God calls you to be a shepherd and does not define the content of your flock.

> You will be a shepherd to some goats as well.

You will be a shepherd to some goats as well. That may not be fun, but it is a fact.

Goats love to mingle with the sheep. I've seen a lot of people who *think* they are sheep but I'm sure are actually goats. God said that you would know them by their fruit. Some people are always into things they shouldn't be in, always have a different point of view (most of the time critical), are the ones often involved in problems, show very little care for the real sheep, are often unreliable and untrustworthy, and do things just for the attention. Wow! Goats are often times very obvious, and for sure, very different.

We fail to see what they can contribute and how they can contribute to the growth of the church. Yet goats have value to the Kingdom. I find it fascinating that the animals referred to the most seem to be the goats and the sheep. When it comes to sacrifice in the Old Testament, in fact, "goat" and the "sacrifice" just seem to go hand and hand. However, it is obvious that God prefers the sheep over the goat.

What Jesus says is very interesting, for He truly defines and clearly describes each person and their outcome, all based on what they produce. Without trying to get too spiritual on you, I will just stick to what it is that He says, okay? I'm not saying this, but Jesus is.

After the "parable of the talents," He says, "And **cast the unprofitable servant** into the **outer darkness**. There will be weeping and gnashing of teeth" (Matthew 25:30).

Oh my goodness! If the American church started to minister from our pulpits this kind of bluntness, maybe there would be great change in God's people...

Verse thirty-one goes on to say that when He comes, Jesus will sit on the throne of His glory. This must mean that the throne is made up of all the "manifested goodness" of the Lord. Where did this goodness come from that was manifested or demonstrated? The sheep on His right hand.

Matthew 25:32-33 says, "*All the nations will be gathered before Him, and He will separate them one from another, as a shepherd divides **his sheep from the goats**. And **He will set the sheep on His right hand, but the goats on the left**.*"

Then Matthew 25:34 says, "*Then the King will say to those on **His right hand**, 'Come, you blessed of My Father, inherit the kingdom prepared for you from the foundation of the world.*" Then verse 41 talks about the left hand. "Then He will also say to those **on the left hand**, 'Depart from Me, you cursed, **into the everlasting fire prepared for the devil and his angels'**" (Matthew 25:41).

Yes, I know, that's a very harsh message. Or is it a great warning to the people of God not to take this salvation too lightly and that we should produce good fruit that builds His throne?

Anyway, there are most likely both sheep and goats in all of our churches.

It is easy to see, because *"you will know them by their fruit."* Also note that they are separated when He comes—not by us today, because that is not our job. Could Jesus be referring to this when He says in Matthew 13:24-30:

> Another parable He put forth to them, saying: "The kingdom of heaven is like a man who sowed good seed in his field; but while men slept, his enemy came and sowed tares among the wheat and went his way. But when the grain had sprouted and produced a crop, then the tares also appeared. So the servants of the owner came and said to him, 'Sir, did you not sow good seed in your field? How then does it have tares?' He said to them, 'An enemy has done this.' The servants said to him, **'Do you want us then to go and gather them up?'**
>
> But he said, 'No, lest while you gather up the tares you also uproot the wheat with them. Let both grow together until the harvest, and at the time of harvest I will say to the reapers, "First gather together the tares and bind them in bundles to burn them, but gather the wheat into my barn." ' "

Sometimes we try to prematurely remove people who we know are goats/tares. I have found that in doing so, I become the bad guy, and I not only lose the goats but also some of their friends that are the real sheep. I had to learn the hard way to just take this to God and let Him fulfill His plan.

Yes, I've removed people—but it is not to be at the expense of the flock of God, the real sheep.

Good Goats

How goats can be good for your church is so important, because it helps you to move wisely and with great caution. Goats can produce in your church—maybe not so much for the Kingdom, but for your plans and for your needs, and they can be very helpful.

Proverbs 27:23,26-27 says,

> *Be diligent to know the state of your flocks, And attend to your herds; The lambs will provide your clothing, **And the goats the price of a field; You shall have enough goats' milk for your food, For the food of your household, And the nourishment of your maidservants.***

Here we see that in the flock there are lambs and goats, and we should know the condition of these people because the sheep and the goats will contribute to the overall plan and desires of the Shepherd.

We have all kinds of people in our church, and you do also—some who adhere to every word that is spoken, and others sleep while the word is being spoken. Sadly, these people who don't show up every week and don't seem to care about much used to be just irritants to my soul. I was not taking into account that they would provide for our church, over and over.

The biggest giver to our church is "loose cash"—the money that someone just throws into the offering buckets. Someone should change their name to Mr. Loose Cash and get a big tax write-off, because each year it is millions of dollars. Economically, we wouldn't make it each year, if not for the people who just throw in their loose cash.

I remember one time being frustrated with the finances of the church. I just blurted out, "If you are not going to tithe, then you're only hurting yourself, so you might as well go buy yourself a hamburger after church."

My smart mouth expressions not only hurt them but also hurt the church. We stopped having enough money to pay all of our bills. Within a few weeks, we were hurting, and I had to repent and ask the people to just put in what you can. The lesson I learned is that we need all the "loose cash" that we can get.

Are they goats? I don't know, and I try not to judge because it is His call at His coming, not *ever* mine. So I could say, thank God for the goats! I'm fed and clothed and have bought fields because of the goats that are mixed into the flock of God. They do provide for us, just as God said.

Chapter 21

Who to Hire and How to Fire

I struggled in this area for years. Hiring can be a lot of fun, but firing someone is never much fun. More often than not, I would fire one person and ten families would leave. What is that all about?

Pastoring is hard enough without the problems that come with hiring and firing, so over the years I found some things that just work to help reduce the collateral damage when you have to let someone go. But let's talk about the fun part first—hiring.

New Workers in the Harvest

In my studies about how Jesus acquired His disciples during His ministry, I recognize some interesting things. First, they had no experience as ministers, and second, their gifting was at times very different, but they all carried a certain kind of heart for the things of God.

In our early years of ministry, hiring was on our minds a lot, for we needed help. But there was always a problem—we had no money to pay for the help that we needed. It seemed that money was the answer to whether or not we hired someone to help or not.

In my natural thinking, it just makes sense to have the money on hand before you hire anyone. That would be just good common sense and wise stewardship. But in the Kingdom, things don't often operate on our common sense from the tree of the knowledge of good and evil.

I remember a time when we were young, and we once again needed some help in the office. Deby and I were doing it all—answering phones, setting appointments, doing the counseling, trying to find volunteers for the children's ministry. We cleaned the washrooms and the toilets each week, as well as vacuuming all the rugs, not to mention ministering God's Word. But we had come to a place where we just couldn't keep on this way. We truly needed help.

How Do You Fire A Volunteer?

But at the heart of our conversation, there were always these words: "we don't have any money." "I know, we will get a volunteer to help," I said. We looked, and it wasn't long before we found someone who could come in once in a while to help. At first that was great, a breath of fresh air. But when we started to give her more responsibilities, she just couldn't handle it. After all, she wasn't paid for what she was doing. And if we ever corrected her, she reminded us that "she was free." And she was right!

We found out that so much time was spent on correcting and training that it just wasn't worth it. The work would be easier just to do it ourselves.

So we were back to the starting place, trying to figure out how to hire someone—someone who could really get the job accomplished. Our volunteer was a kind person but was not what we needed to help us get this overwhelming job done.

As you know, painting yourself into a corner is not a very good place to be. We need someone good, and we didn't want to hire our volunteer, so how did we tell her? When she volunteered, in the back of her mind, she was hoping that it might turn into a paying job. We had no idea that she was thinking that or we would have gone in a different direction. So the big question was what was going to happen when we didn't hire her, and how would she react to this new plan—a plan that does not include her?

We had to make a decision in order to move forward. We still did not have the money to hire anyone, but we had to anyway, or we were not going to make it.

When the Bible says *"the just shall live by faith,"* we must recognize what is truly being said. It is not just to live by faith for a while but for the rest of our natural lives on this earth.

We got up the courage to tell her that it was time for us to hire a full-time employee. She looked at us and said, "Okay, how much do you want to pay me?" Our hearts sank, but somehow we got up the courage and said, "Sorry, we think for our needs that we need to hire someone else. It just didn't work out the way we all hoped it would, and we think that there is someone out there that can get the job done easier than you."

Immediately, we went from being her loving pastors to Satan's brother and sister. And of course, she left the church and immediately took about a dozen people with her.

That solved the problem of needing to hire more help because by the time she was finished, we had lost a lot of people and were not so busy anymore!

What a lousy experience! We thought that there must be a way of doing this without stopping the move of God that you are trying to protect by hiring someone to help.

Who Works for Whom?

The next time it was very different. We hired a person who was very talented. She seemed to be perfect for getting the job done but had one flaw—after a while, it felt like *we* were working for *her*. Somehow in our excitement of having someone who could perform, we complimented her too much and it went to her head. She thought of herself as the "great leader" of the church, and she made us feel that she had control of everything—including us!

Maybe she was right. She had control of us because she handled the books, and whoever controls the money controls the ministry. At least that's what she thought. We had to pull back some of her authority and take control of the ministry back. It wasn't pleasant, but it had to be done. And she got in line.

The Faithful Few

Over the many years that we have had to go through the horrors of firing people, it has always been an experience that I don't look forward to (notice how I said "I"—that's because Deby runs for the hills during this time).

Some years back, the economy got really bad, and the church was hemorrhaging money to the tune of hundreds of thousands of dollars each month. We just needed to let some people go. We had a staff of about 125 people, and we identified about twenty-two that we needed to let go. It was truly no fault of theirs; it was only because we needed to reduce our monthly expenses and try to ride out the economic storm. I hated it, and we did all we could to help them collect unemployment and find other jobs.

It just wasn't enough. They disliked us, and all left the church—except for one person. When it was time to rehire, he was the only one we rehired because he was **faithful**. A new concept for us was being birthed in our souls—hire people who remain faithful.

That's what Jesus found inside His disciples. It's not easy to find someone who will remain faithful during tough times. The best employees are the ones that you do not have to fire but may need to be let go. They will remain faithful to their church and trust their pastors. Even when the pastors have to make a tough call, they respect them and trust them enough not to leave the church and take others with them out of revenge.

The Pain of Letting Go

More than once, I had to let a pastor go. This can become a real problem because it becomes obvious to the church and can cause some instability to those that know and love them. When they started, they seemed so kind and faithful, but over the years, something changed. There was no longer an excitement and challenge associated with their position. You could just feel that it had become a hireling situation. What a shame. Was it me, or the ministry, or maybe the reality of the ministry? I don't know. It just happens.

Some of the pastors had a dislike and disrespect towards us. We were no longer flowing together but were growing further and further apart until there was no other choice but to let them go.

The concern is if I let this pastor go, it could turn out to be a big problem, for he is not just an office worker but someone of influence in our church. And when this big tree falls, he might take out a lot of people with him. So I start the process of trying to restore the "wayward" pastor. It has never worked, but it shows God's heart that will always call for change before the gavel comes down.

> Showing God's heart, His kindness, and His mercy is exactly what God expects from His leaders.

Showing God's heart, His kindness, and His mercy is exactly what God expects from His leaders.

This is not an easy time for us pastors and not an easy time for the pastor who is going to lose his job, not to mention his family and his ego. Before I let him go, I must show mercy (I know that God is watching me on how I handle this). It becomes the very characteristic of a godly decision. Before you let anyone go, there must be mercy expressed, *before and after* you make the call.

If you want God's presence in your decision, then you are going to have to show some of His fruit in your actions.

When it is time to let him go, some things must again take place. As much as it pains us, we must think about him and his family. Oh, I know what you are thinking—he wasn't thinking of my family or the family of God when he was disloyal, dysfunctional, or disobedient. So why would I think about his family? We are not moved by what others do or don't do; we must be moved by what Jesus wants us to be moved by.

When Judas was disloyal, Jesus fed him, washed his feet, and kissed him. He showed kindness and mercy to the traitor Judas. It is just what God does. Probably no one we have to fire or let go will ever be as bad as Judas.

Somehow we think that the termination of a bad employee must be without kindness and blessings. Like the world, we see ourselves as hard and tough. But, in the Kingdom, it is very different. A lesson learned is the most valuable lesson of all.

When I finally had no other choice, and I had to let an influential pastor go, I called him into my office and told him of my decision. He stared at me with great hate in his eyes; I could feel the desire for revenge and that he wanted to come after me. But then I expressed some "care," and it changed everything. Love never fails.

I told him that I cared about him and his family and that I was truly sorry that all has come to this but it must be done. I expressed that I was not going to give him the typical two weeks salary as a severance pay; I was going to give him *six months* of full severance pay. This would help him to have time to find another job and help him to make the transition back to the new workplace. This pastor and others for which I've used this strategy have all have been very grateful.

And that is when I explained that this offer came with some requirements that must be fulfilled if he were to receive a monthly check for the next six months.

#1 If I hear one negative remark about this church or the leadership during the next six months that can be traced back to him, all further checks will stop.

#2 He must leave the church and is not allowed to contact anyone or the checks will stop. If anyone asked him why he left, he was to explain there was just a difference of opinions.

#3 He could not start a church within forty-five miles of our church during the six months. (They all say they wouldn't do that, but they all do. But after six months, they are no longer an influence in my church, so there is minimal effect on us.)

#4 He can never prospect for new church members from our church or the checks stop.

Let me tell you, this works so well, you just won't believe it. No backlash, no trouble.

Consider Mercy

The second thing that I would have you to think about is *mercy*. When it comes to "how to fire," keeping God involved in your ministry is the most important thing that you can do. God is not into hurting anyone, nor is He going to be unkind to anyone. You must think about the family and the feelings of others.

> No more sacrificing people for the benefit of the ministry!

You may get away with being unkind now, but someday you will have to report to Him.

No more sacrificing people for the benefit of the ministry! It just doesn't work that way; it is not the heart of God.

I have found that the more mercy I give, the more the Lord is pleased. Many times, these people who are going to be let go don't deserve any mercy (in our thinking), but God is not looking for who deserves it or not but only that all receive it. That is what mercy is all about.

Thank God that our future is not based on what we deserve but is in the hand of a merciful God.

When you have to fire someone, make sure you season this hard act with kindness and great generosity. Do this for your own sake, for the person getting fired, and, most importantly, your God. Now the bad experience becomes a good experience. Remember what I mean by "good."

Who to Hire

So to just give you the right thinking about "who to hire and how to fire," do *not* focus on hiring the person with the most talent or gifting or education, even though that is all very important.

If I was hiring for a position in the world, this is all that I would use to make my decision. But I'm in the church. It is a completely different set of rules—God's rules and Gods ways—and we often miss the most important characteristic of all, and that is FAITHFULNESS. I use faithfulness as the measure of character for the non-platform employee. I found that when a person is faithful, they will find out how to develop the skill level to do the job.

Now, when it comes to employees who will minister from the platform, gifting has to be considered. You wouldn't want to hire a music minister to lead worship from the platform without some ability to sing or play. Gifting is very important, but it is not everything! There should be a calling along with the gifting. If they are not faithful, or if they are not called to your ministry, it will end up in a big disaster.

Talent and gifting become the goal of the faithful, and it is not long before you have not only the talent, the gifting, and skill set to do the job but also a person who *remains* faithful. Now that is what you need for a great team!

By the way, faithfulness is not something that is defined by time, like one or two years; it is defined by the heart. It is a lifetime commitment to what God has for you to do. If there should be a change of heart, you will know.

God Loves Faithfulness

I remember this story of a minister who realized that she needed faithfulness in her ministry. At first, she didn't know how to identify when an employee was faithful. She talked to God about it, but got no real clear answer. This condition continued; she felt that most of the people who worked for her were just onboard because of the paycheck.

So one day she gathered her twenty employees all together and told them that she was having money trouble and would have to let them all go. All twenty packed up their stuff and left the office. After a week went by, one of her former employees who had been in a low-level office position showed up and asked if she could come back to work. She wasn't expecting to be paid; she just loved working in her ministry because it was her way to serve the Lord. It wasn't about the money for her.

The minister was so excited that someone would truly follow God and be faithful, no matter if she got paid or not. It wasn't long before she hired her back with full pay and a promotion to office manager. For the rest of her life in the ministry, this new office manager out-performed all previous employees. She was faithful first; then the talent and gifting came. She was outstanding in every area. What made her any different? Simple—God loved to work with her because God loves the faithful.

Chapter 22

The Generous Pastor

All too often, we run our churches like the world runs a business. Money and bottom lines often speak louder than the voice of the Lord when it comes to making the right choices for our ministries. This shouldn't be what we hear, but it is.

Often times, we don't even recognize that we follow business principles more than godly principles. Of course, no one will admit this, simply because if we recognize it, then we would, in good conscience, change it.

Most people's lives are controlled by money. Some ministries experience financial abundance and get lazy. They feel they are doing good because their carnal-minded board members look at the bottom line, since that's what they do in their successful businesses. Other ministries have no real money to be generous with. This, of course, gives us a good excuse for not doing much. There is a third scenario, however, and it is when the finances of the church are misdirected to some other form of ministry that costs so much that it takes the very heart of generosity out of the church.

Whatever financial condition we find ourselves in, this is a worthy subject. Why? Because our God is very generous—very, very generous.

For God so loved the world that He *what*? Of course, *"gave."* A ministry must represent Him, His wants, His will, His plan, His character, and His nature, which is generosity. That is who He is and what He does. He is a giver in every area and in every form. How could we expect this generous God to be a part of our church if we don't represent Him properly? The crossroad for all of us is in how much we believe this. And, of course, what we are going to do about it. **This will define your future.**

We ministers teach year after year about finances, and we should. But how much more do the principles of finance and stewardship apply to the church? The Word of God on finances is not just to the people so that the church can have money, but also for a lesson on what the church itself should be acting like. The people are generous when the church first becomes generous.

Often times we have that backward. We say, "We will become generous if we have the money." That is like saying, "Fireplace, give me heat; then I'll put in the wood." It just doesn't work like that—for the people or for the church. We all have to put in the wood first, then comes the heat.

Generosity does not come *after* you get the money. Money comes and follows the act of generosity. The principle is that the act comes first, then God gets involved in the act. You must sow first, then you reap. You don't reap first then you sow. We often forget this simple truth.

God Does Generosity

I had this backward for years, thinking, "God, when you give me the money, then I'll be generous." Generosity is what God does, and it is who God is. **Ephesians 3:20 says, "*Now to Him who is able to do exceedingly abundantly above all that we ask or think, according to the power that works in us.*"**

Generosity is the overflow to someone's needs. It is that amount that goes beyond the normal to meet the needs of someone else.

Some of the pastors that I have known over the years have had their ministries stifled because they have not addressed the root of this problem—worry. Just as simple as that: worry can stop your whole ministry.

Worry is the outpouring of a lack of faith, because the proof of faith is rest.

I have talked to some of these pastors and mentioned to them that I think that a little word called worry has popped up in their life. When asked what it is that they are worried about, they almost always say that they aren't worried—they just have "a concern."

> Worry is the outpouring of a lack of faith, because the proof of faith is rest.

Here is what many do not see—concerns are okay and very natural. But when the concern hangs around too long, it becomes worry, worry attacks your faith, and you become a double-minded man. And the Bible says that you won't be getting anything from God.

James 1:5-8 tells us,

> *If any of you lacks wisdom, let him ask of God, who gives to all liberally and without reproach, and it will be given to*

him. But let him ask in faith, with no doubting, for he who doubts is like a wave of the sea driven and tossed by the wind. For let not that man suppose that he will receive anything from the Lord; he is a double-minded man, unstable in all his ways.

You deal with worry the same way that you deal with any other problem—by casting your cares onto Jesus **and leaving them there.** *"Therefore humble yourselves under the mighty hand of God, that He may exalt you in due time, casting all your care upon Him, for He cares for you"* (1 Peter 5:6-7).

Generosity Is The Antidote to Covetousness

In Luke 12:15 it says, *"And He said to them, 'Take heed and beware of covetousness, for one's life does not consist in the abundance of the things he possesses.'"* Covetousness is the strong desire and passion for something other than God. At times it can become the very thing that controls us. Then, as you know, it can turn into an idol. After that comes great loss of your ministry.

> Generosity is seeing a need and doing all that you can to fulfill it.

Generosity helps to keep you dependent and reliant on God for all things. It will bring great health to your efforts as a church.

Let me define how generosity works in ministry: generosity is seeing a need and doing all that you can to fulfill it. As simple as that. Being able to see a *true* need is a gift from God, because there are people who are very needy around you all the time.

In our church, there are more people in need of help than there are people or money to help. There is always someone who has requested something. And I must tell you the truth, we do not meet the needs of everybody, because if we tried to do that, we wouldn't last long as a church. But there is the heartfelt desire of the Holy Spirit that from time to time cries out to meet that need. We look for that heartfelt desire, and we do all we can to fill it.

I have always thought of the church as a big tree with arms that reach out like the limbs of the tree. This tree has a trunk and a root system that must remain healthy or the tree will die off. And what good is a dead tree or church?

When an arm reaches out, hey, that is great—but not to the place where the weight of the limb pulls out the root. I really wanted to get involved in and be generous toward many things that were presented to me over the years, but I saw that it could be unhealthy for the church (the root).

Knowing when to give and who to give to is a very godly thing ("good"). It takes great godly insight to keep your generosity on the right track. There are people who God wants you to get involved with, and there are people who you will want to get involved with, but it is not always God.

Generosity can be a God thing, but poor stewardship can be a trap that stops the plan of God for your church. If you train yourself to hear and follow God's leading in all areas of your ministry, why wouldn't you want to get directions from God as to who and what to be generous toward?

Generosity doesn't happen because you have extra money in the bank; generosity comes because you have heard from God. You may not have any extra money, but you will do as God has said. And that will take faith.

Missions

I believe in missions. Missions are a very important part of the church and should be an outreach to someone else who is doing a work that you can't do in a place that you maybe don't want to go.

Things have changed over the years, and many pastors consider themselves, and the work that they do, as their missions program. I'm not sure that qualifies as missions with God; maybe it does. But for me, missions are *missions*, and that requires that I do all I can do to help support someone else in their work in a place I am not going.

In a church like ours, there seems to be someone each week that wanted to meet with me at the back door to talk to me about what they are doing—and of course the reason for that is that they are looking for support. Who then is God wanting me to support?

I found myself in a dilemma. I loved them all and wanted to get involved with all of them. They are doing a work that I do not want to do. I'm happy at my church.

One time I went on a missions trip with a missionary. When I got home, I wrote a personal note of thanks, and said, "Thank you so much for inviting me to go along. Please never invite me again." He thought it was funny and carried it in his Bible for a laugh from time to time.

I felt that my job was to encourage the missionaries. Believe me when I say they do a better job than I will ever do. In the same thinking, I'll do a better job in the church than maybe they could. We should encourage people to continue doing their calling, and not with just words but with economic support. I can't always do that; I don't have that much money, and it could pull out the root. So I must listen for His approval for my involvement.

Missionaries are so special to me. While I'm home in my comfortable bed, eating good food, or enjoying the day at Disneyland with my grandchildren, missionaries often times live in very poor conditions and with not many benefits in their lives so that they can tell someone about Jesus. These saints are the real heroes of the faith. To be truthful, when I think about them, I wonder if I am even saved. Thank God for His grace!

These wonderful saints wait to talk to me after church so they might get some financial help. It just does not make much sense that God would allow us pastors to be the stewards of His finances and carry the responsibility of giving to the right ones. We don't have a lot of money, so what we have must be given correctly and considered generous by God. If not, then we become bad stewards of His resources. And that spells out trouble for our future.

Beware Taking Advantage of Missionaries

I have heard of how we pastors take advantage of missionaries, using them for personal gain, thinking that our ministries are so important and others are less important. Truth be known, all ministries are important to God. When we think contrary to this, it stops God from doing what we want Him to do.

I have a dear friend in the remote part of the world doing the work of an apostle. He and his wife have started many churches with the indigenous people. He has truly changed the thinking and the hearts of that very obscure place. Wow, what a great man of God!

He recently told me a story of a very famous pastor who came to see him. This pastor brought a large video team with him, all to document what was happening there in this outer edge of the world.

The visiting pastor was invited to minister and be a participant in the ongoing ministry of this missionary. The cameras were all set up, and they worked very hard to capture as much footage as they could.

The surprise came when the video team was only taking pictures of the famous pastor while he did ministry. I don't have any problem with that. I'm sure he was going back to his church to show how this missions ministry is doing. What troubled me came when I asked if this pastor was a regular supporter of this missionaries ministry. His answer shocked me: "No, he has never given a thing." Now that to me is a perfect example of a stingy spirit that is just out for itself. Then Romans 14:4 kicked in. Who am I to judge? So I'm learning to shut my mouth.

When you are just out for yourself, God is not in it. You are truly by yourself without His presence, and it won't be long before your ministry fails.

I know that God is into a true heart of generosity. If you're generous in ministry, you will never have to worry that God won't meet your needs or that your ministry might fail. Never, never will you fail.

Isaiah 32:8 promises, *"But a generous man devises generous things, **And by generosity he shall stand.**"*

Proverbs 11:24-25 tells us, *"There is one who scatters, yet increases more; And there is one who withholds more than is right, But it leads to poverty. The generous soul will be made rich, **And he who waters will also be watered himself.**"*

> Generosity is not always giving. Sometimes, it could be just not taking something.

Take Less, Give More

Generosity is not always giving. Sometimes, it could be just not taking something.

We don't always think of someone who doesn't *take* something as being generous. One time—just once—there was a person who ministered at our church. After giving of himself all weekend, he wouldn't receive the honorarium. I strongly encouraged him, but I couldn't get him to take the offering. Instead of it being a good thing, it was insulting to my foolish mind. I gave him all the scriptures I could to try to convince him to take the honorarium, but nothing worked. At the time, I didn't see him as generous, but as I grew in maturity, I could see that this person was a very, very generous man.

A couple set up an appointment to come in and see me about a problem they were having in their business. When we got around to the problem, it was about money. They just couldn't pay their bills because they didn't have enough money.

We started to talk about the profit and the loss of the business. When I found out how much money they made in the first half of the year, I was surprised. "Where did all the money go?" I asked. Their answer floored me: "We gave about 80% of our income to the church."

"Well," I said, "That's an easy fix—stop it, and if you bring in the tithe, 10%, that would be a blessing to all." They thought that the more they gave, the more God would bless them. I then explained to them that you can't give someone else's money away and see that as generous. The money they gave belonged to the people they owed.

In my heart, I could hear the Lord say, "Give them back their money." I knew that we didn't have a lot of money and were just barely making it. That must be the devil talking to me, I thought. How were we going to make it if I gave back what they have given over the last six months?

I called our accounting department and asked how much this couple had given—it was somewhere in the neighborhood of $60,000. When I did the math in my head, I was sick. But, I knew it was God. And God said it, so I'm going to do it.

I told the accounting department to keep $6,000 and to write a check for $54,000.00 to this couple. The accounting department mentioned to me that we had already spent this money paying our bills over the last six months. I determined that if we were going to go broke because we were generous, then we would go broke.

We did not, and God supplied all of our needs. **Generosity will test your faith.**

When we were a smaller church of about 350 people, a man came into the office and introduced himself to me. He was a pastor of a church about a mile down the road. He said that when we moved into the area, he started to lose people from his church, and he thought they were coming to my church. He said that the people who visit His church now don't stay because they feel uncomfortable; it had become such a small group that they felt that his church had no value and wouldn't stay.

He went on to ask me the most challenging question of my ministry—would I consider sending some people to his church so that the new people didn't feel so out of place? While I'm sitting there listing to his request, I'm thinking to myself, "This guy is nuts. I'll give up money, or about anything else, but don't touch the people, not the people." I'm thinking there is no way I'll send people from our church to his. What if they stayed or maybe gave their money *there*?

I didn't know what to say. I asked him how many and for how long. I've worked hard for each person, and now this man wanted me to send them to his church? I would be nuts to say yes to this request. And that would make me a bigger nut than even him!

In my heart, the issue was already settled. I could hardly wait until he stopped talking just to say "No." As I sat there with a smug look on my face and a smug answer in my heart, God spoke to me, "I want you to do it." *What*! I thought that must be the devil talking to me. I wanted to say "Get behind me Satan!" But after I settled down, I knew it was God.

God was telling me that I was in a covetous position with the people, and I needed to break the back of this idolatry. I do not like it when He is so right and so blunt.

Colossians 3:5 says, "*Therefore put to death your members which are on the earth: fornication, uncleanness, passion, evil desire, **and covetousness, which is idolatry.***" Remember, covetousness is an overwhelming desire for someone or something that is not God. If continued, it will become a form of idolatry. And I was there. I was challenged beyond my logic.

I told that pastor that I couldn't make people do it, but I could present it to the people and explain the reasoning. The first week, about four couples went, and they stayed for about four weeks, then came back home. I announced it every week for a month.

I was free of that idolatry, and all the people in time came back to our church.

His church did pick up a few families that stopped by to visit. And he started to grow again—but not with our people but new ones. They ended up buying a church building and to this day are healthy in ministry.

Generosity can and should operate on many different levels. Generosity will build you, or it can break you. Building you up comes when you're generous, and the breaking you down comes when you're not generous.

I don't believe that you can be too generous. If I err, may it be for being too generous.

Chapter 23:

Fishing Without Bait

It's just crazy how much we pastors want our churches to grow. We are happy and on top of the world when they grow. (I'm talking about the numbers of people that attend our churches. There are all kinds of growth we could be talking about, but I'm talking about numerically.)

As I said before, it is just a God thing that is built into the heart of the pastors, and it is so clear that pastors want to have their churches grow. I've met only a few pastors over the years who said they don't care if their churches grow or not. But if I were a betting man, I would bet that deep down inside, they really wanted it, and they were just saying that to sound spiritual. We all play that game from time to time.

There are so many things that cause a church to grow, but the bottom line is this: "**Unless the LORD builds the house, They labor in vain who build it;** Unless the LORD guards the city, The watchman stays awake in vain" (Psalm 127:1).

This verse is clear—the Lord builds His churches. I am not saying that you're to sit around and do nothing. God uses men and women to build His church, and this effort needs to be under His direction, guidance, pleasure, and plan. Or, as I've said before, He just won't get involved in it as much as He could.

I have seen so many people who don't do much to build His church. When questioned, their answer would sound something like, "If He wants to build it, He will." Well, that's great, and it sounds good, but it is only a partial truth. God says that if you don't sow, don't expect to reap. So, we could say if He wants a harvest that He will just make a harvest, and we don't have to sow. But that is not what His Word says—someone must sow.

I truly believe that God doesn't do much by Himself, and it is obvious that we are not to operate without Him. This is the way that it works—I put in the best natural effort I can, He puts in His super effort, and we come up with a "supernatural" effort. That is what it is going to take to get our churches to grow.

The big question is how do I play out my part?

Our Part—Work Hard

First, I come to a humble (dependent) position in God. It may sound like this: "Lord, I know you want my church to grow and reach more people, and I want my church to grow and reach more people. Therefore, show me how." It may take the rest of your life in ministry, but if you're in tune with Him, He will show you what it is that He wants from you. Like I said before, you are not allowed to just follow others, you are to learn to hear from Him and follow His lead. This is followship.

The result is a word we all want to see in our churches, "momentum," and the church grows. It just grows and grows.

I titled this chapter Fishing Without Bait for a very important reason. Bait is what we use to catch fish. I hope you are a fisherman, because if you're a pastor, you're also a fisher of men.

Like any fisherman will tell you, your bait has got to be the right kind of bait, and at the right timing, and at the right place. Without bait, you might just starve to death waiting to snag a fish with just your hook. Sometimes I feel that many churches just snag a person from time to time and seem to be satisfied with that effort. Maybe the pastors just don't know that there is a better way.

When you are a good fisherman, you will make every effort to catch fish. It all really works like this: the bigger the effort, the bigger the catch (in terms of amount).

You will study the right equipment and the right times and places to fish. You will go to bed early the night before in order not to be too tired, you will get up before the sun comes up and even drive for hours to be at the right spot at the right time. Before the others start to show up, you will have already caught a bunch. The principle is the one who works the hardest is usually the one who catches the most fish.

> I'm reminded that Paul, the "least apostle," worked harder than anyone!

It is the same with God and His people.

The Right Bait

Wrong bait brings wrong results. When I was a young trout fisherman, and I would see a person catching lots of fish, I would try to get up close to find out what it was that they were using.

Often times I could see what bait they were using. But most of the time I just had to humble myself and ask, "Hey, you're doing great, what are you using?" Most of the time they would answer, but sometimes they just ignored me.

Getting the right bait was worth the embarrassment of being ignored. It all translated to fish, and, after all, fish were why I was there.

People are why you're there as a pastor, and truth be known, your job is to catch them. We try and we pray, but there are times when nothing seems to work. Let us try some "fresh bait."

Recently I saw something that took me years to learn. When our church was at the highest attendance, we were doing something very special. **We were having lots of events.**

Events are special activities in the church that are over and above the regular church services. These events brought in people to our church.

Lots of people would come to the event and would just be visiting. But so much more would take place in their lives. Many were saved, many found the church they were looking for, and many simply stay and continue to come to church because they just got comfortable.

This gave the people, those who already attended the church, a reason and an easy way to invite people that would not normally come to church. I found that after visitors came a few times, many became so involved that they saw our church as their church and started to come over and over. Families became familiar with the church. They had a good time, and they already had friends in the church. What could be better?

Some events were better than others. In the old days, we would have an event for almost everything. We would have church plays at least once or even twice per year. Someone would write a play with lots of actors and sets that would be made in-house. No one could act in the play who did not go to our church, because the more people who acted in the production, the more people the crew and actors invited. Keep in mind that we weren't using professionals, just people in the church who wanted to do something for Jesus.

Many people would never come to church because though church was not their thing; when they were invited to an event, they came.

Sometimes over a two to three week period of time, we might have some extra 10,000 people visiting our church. Who gets 10,000 people coming to visit a church in a few weeks? We would always give an aggressive altar call and would have thousands respond! They didn't all come back, but at least there is a spiritual connection with our church. And we were that connection for a church in their lives. It was a good experience for them and us, and when they were ready to start going to church, we were in their thoughts.

Some people hire actors to come in and do the Christian plays, but I found that when that happened, our people didn't invite as many people to the play. They came out, but they did not aggressively invite the relatives and friends. A very different dynamic took place when the actors and set builders were all from the church. They wanted it to be successful, so they would all work hard to get others to come. It became their ministry effort.

Were the plays top quality? No, but that is what made them fun and alive, and it became a great experience for all. (By the way, they were always Christian stories that told of Jesus.)

We never replaced our church services with a play. Church services are something that honors God and builds His people. We did not want to treat our services as common, because it would be an insult to God. The people would feel as if the service was just another thing and start to treat our services as common. All the plays were on nights that we had no services, except for Sunday night. It was a night that we could get more people together.

An "event" is something that happens at church, not somewhere else. Many times people suggested that we should hold the event in a better venue "off campus." I always said no, because I wanted the visitors to be in our church and not in some other place. For me, the whole object was to get them into our building and have a great experience so that they know where to go to church.

The event was not about the play but about church growth and evangelism. We were giving the people who went to our church a platform for invitation. That is the purpose of an event.

Celebrate!

An event is also a church-wide celebration for some reason or another. We celebrated everything, all the time.

The employees got a little frustrated from time to time, because they were the ones that did all the work for the celebration and even after, but we gave them lots of time off because of all the extra time they put in. Oh, by the way, if I asked them if they want to work extra long and hard for an event celebration to happen, most would say, "We just did an event," or "I think this year we should pass." I found out that if I listened to them, then we would have an employee-run church instead of a God-run church. It is just part of our jobs to bring the people into a place of celebration.

Have you ever noticed how many celebrations God's people were required to be a part of in the Old Testament? Many! Because God

wanted His experience with His people to
be exciting. They gathered, and they had
a party with food and music and dancing,
just a time of celebration. It became a time
of people and love and appreciation, just a
godly release of tension and great fellowship with people that are like-thinkers.

> God wanted His
> experience with
> His people to
> be exciting.

One of our celebrations is a time of year
when the church should celebrate more than any other—Christmas.
"Christmas" is a taboo word in most American churches. For some
of you, you're now judging me and asking yourselves something
like, "Doesn't he know that that is just a pagan holiday that celebrates the wrong stuff?" We know all the excuses that people make
so they do not have to have a celebration.

We live in a time when the "Christ of Christmas" is being removed
from everything and every where. It has now become a holiday
time of year, or winter break time, all with no acknowledgment of
Jesus. You have got to be kidding!

This time of the year must be set aside by the church to celebrate
the birth of our Savior. We all know that He wasn't born on the
25th of December, but that should not keep us from celebrating
His birth.

We start each Christmas season by explaining why we need to
celebrate His birth and even the reasons why some people choose
not to. As a church, we are not celebrating the evergreen tree and
the goddess of fertility. We don't celebrate the lights or the bulbs
on the trees, but we as a church are celebrating the life of our Lord
and Savior.

Our celebration lasts for as long as three weeks. We have lots of
lights and Christmas trees, music, songs, food, and amazing plays

with great dance teams. We also have great messages about Jesus and His birth, the great faith of Mary and Joseph, John and Elizabeth, and others. It's never exactly the same each year because each year God gives us fresh revelations.

Thousands came from all over to see the church and be a part of the celebration. They are not going to get it somewhere else. We see thousands get saved during our three weeks of Christmas celebrations. And after the first of the year, many start to come to church to be spiritually fed.

Opportunities for Celebration

Celebrations and events are fishing with the right bait.

Have you ever thought about how many celebrations your church could have during a year? I bet you haven't. How about Easter? I'm not talking about just one day of Easter, but two maybe three weeks of resurrection celebration. It is a big thing that happened for us, and we should make it a very big thing in the hearts of our people and the many people that visit.

How about a celebration of freedom? The 4th of July is a great time to celebrate our freedom as a country and as a Christian. Who wouldn't want to come out for free hot dogs and ice cream along with dancing and music and maybe your own fireworks show?

One celebration that brings thousands out is our Harvest Carnival that takes the place of Halloween, a truly pagan holiday. We want to light a candle in the midst of all that darkness, and we want our children safe. We also want to use this time to familiarize others with our church. This becomes one of the great outreaches of the year. Lots of candy, popcorn, jump houses, games, rides, and so much more draw families in. And the Word of God is preached everywhere, with lots of altar calls.

Celebrate your church's birthday. We just had a birthday party for the church, and somewhere between 5,000-7,000 people came. There was lots of food and dancing and music and all the ice cream the kids can eat—free of course. I would say I had never seen at least one-third of the people before.

Outreach, celebration, and events bring growth to your church.

Keep it Real

How do you pay for all of this? There is always enough money for celebrations because it is the will of God. Never let money be the deciding factor of whether or not you will celebrate. Money should not make that decision, only God and your faith that backs what He says. And by the way, when God is in something, then *He* will pay for it. He will show you how to make it all work through Him.

Just a little warning: **your personal birthday or your wedding anniversary is not a celebration.** I've seen some churches celebrate the pastor more than the real events that bring glory to God. Stop it! Get off yourself and get to the real celebration of Jesus in your church. People want and need to know about Jesus and not you. Get out of the way and bring real life to your church.

When you fish with bait, the real bait of Jesus, fish bite and you catch fish. Isn't that why Jesus made Peter "a fisher of men"? When did the church get off track and start just to have *services*?

When church operates right, it becomes a whole lot more than a service; it becomes an encounter with God—something that stirs the spirit and brings people face to face with the living Christ. We want encounters that will so impress upon the hearts of people that they will not be able to shake off God's presence for days.

Someone once said that I manipulate the people. Well, my response to that is this—*YES!* I do all I can and in every way. The enemy does everything he can to stop and to manipulate the people not to be around Jesus or to hear anything about Him. We preachers should just play fair and influence people for Jesus, and when Lucifer stops, then maybe, just maybe, we should stop. But until then, we should be doing anything and everything to persuade people to consider Christ in a very aggressive way.

I have found that the dumbest parents in the world are parents who tell their children that they can decide which way they want to go with God when they grow up. The enemy does everything he can to stop them from ever thinking about God. Would you call that evil manipulation? I would, and by the way, it is the will of God that parents teach their children about God. What I do is "godly influencing." You can call it "manipulation" if you want to, but God is pleased with it. The proof is in the pudding—lots of people getting saved, and lots of lives being changed.

I have found that pastors who don't go after the souls of men are pastors who don't have as healthy of a church as they could have, and some "godly manipulation" might help build the Kingdom of God. I know it would please God. So the question is, "Are we men-pleasers or are we God-pleasers?" Your call.

Bring On the Fresh Bait

When I was a young boy, my father would take my brother and me fishing. It all started days before, where Dad would go through how to fish, and even how to bait the hook. He often would go through our tackle box and see what kind of bait we had and make sure we also had the right size leaders and hooks. I remember that Dad was a great fisherman who always caught lots of fish.

Sometimes he would ask me where I got my bait. If I told him it was left over from last season, then he would tell me to throw it out. He always said that old bait is no good, and we would pick up some fresh bait for our trip.

Old bait won't work, and it is time for some of you to check your tackle box and refresh with some new ideas that catch lots of fish. In the State of California the limit is five trout, but with God there is no limit.

Try something new. We have about 150 guests come to our church services each month. But a good event/celebration could bring in 10,000 people. What a difference! I never read about Jesus having the fisherman use poles; He always had them use nets. The best bait is actually a net because it catches the most fish.

The Importance of an Aggressive Altar Call

I realized very quickly that you can't do anything in and of yourself. The blessing in my ministry has been because of God's faithfulness and grace, not my own strengths. Let me give you some background about what happened in our church.

> I realized very quickly that you can't do anything in and of yourself.

We had grown to about 250 people on a good Sunday. I was preaching with every bit of vigor and vim that you can imagine. Yet I was so discouraged about winning souls. My wonderful wife Deby, who has supported me through the years, was bugging me about the altar call. I kept saying to her that I was not an evangelist but a Bible teacher. In fact, I hid behind the fact that in my many trips to Africa I was probably the only guy in the world that could go there, have thousands attend, give an altar call, and not one person would respond. Not one! It just proved that I wasn't a soul winner, right? Not necessarily.

Perhaps you have felt similar. In my church, I would preach a great message, and the people would be with me, but when I gave an altar call, it was like I threw a wet blanket all over the crowd. Everyone would leave discouraged. When people leave discouraged, it's hard to get them to come back.

I told Deby that I couldn't get anybody saved. She continued to pray for me and told me that I needed to keep doing altar calls. I even put a bold, colorful note "Altar Call" at the end of my sermon notes because I would forget to give one without the note.

I was told that if you preach the Word of God, people will just come. I have found that is simply not true! I preached the Word of God, and they still did not come. Some people even left complaining and calling us names. I would see others at the back door as they were leaving who would tell me that our church was the greatest they had ever been to…but then they never came back. I must be doing something wrong, I thought.

From A Trickle to A Roar

I began to give altar calls at every service, and months passed without anyone responding. Eventually, *one person* came forward for salvation. I was so thrilled! Soon after that, we had two people come forward to receive Jesus. Today, years later, it is not unusual to see hundreds of people get saved in our weekend services. Our church went from 250 to 10,000 people in a little under a decade and kept growing to over 20,000 in two decades. It all started with what I call an "aggressive, in your face" altar call.

People now say I am an evangelist with an anointing for getting people saved. No, I am a pastor in love with people, and I had to learn how to give an altar call. You too can also win people to the

Lord when you learn how and why you should give an aggressive altar call.

I was visiting a church with a congregation of at least 6,000 people. There were about 2,500 adults in the audience. The pastor preached a great message and said this for the altar call: "If you're here today and you would like to get saved, know more about this church, need the baptism of the Holy Spirit or want to be healed, I want you to get out of your seat and come forward." I thought, "That's horrible!" Out of that large crowd, only fifteen people came forward. A couple of them might have come forward to get saved. Some may have been filled with the Holy Spirit. In my heart, I felt that there was a minimum of 250 people who needed salvation. They did not have an aggressive altar call, and those people left that day without becoming right with God.

In another meeting, a speaker gave a great altar call, but nobody responded. So she jumped out of the salvation altar call and went to the baptism of the Holy Spirit, where four or five people responded. Once again, I believe that because there was no response, she gave up too quickly and went to the other topics where she could get a response. I believe we give up much too easily. We are afraid of what people think of us. We become uncomfortable and do not want to look bad in front of the people, so we give up on what we should be doing and do what makes us look better before the people. Keep in mind that all these feelings come from the tree in the Garden.

When the Lord is pleased, He brings people— lots of them.

Fear of failure keeps a pastor from giving an aggressive altar call as he should. Be prepared to be made a spectacle for Jesus. If we are afraid of the people or what we look like in front of the people, then this will not work. We need to be more afraid of God than people! We need to do what pleases the Lord. And when the Lord is pleased, *He* brings people—lots of them.

I told God that I would give an altar call at any meeting where I ministered. Just put people in front of me, and I'll give it. I believe God taught me how to give an effective altar call because of this commitment.

One minister came to me and asked if would come and speak to his church's leadership, a large group of ninety-five people. I ministered at their breakfast meeting, and the pastor invited me to share in the afternoon as well. As I was sharing with them in the afternoon, God spoke to me and said, "Give them an altar call." I said, "Lord, this is the leadership of his church!" Nevertheless, I obeyed and gave an altar call after my message. Forty-two people out of the ninety-five people in leadership responded to accept Jesus! If that wasn't shocking enough, the pastor got pretty angry! He said, "Listen here! Those are my leaders, counselors, and ushers. They count my offerings!" I responded, "Do they go to heaven because they usher people into your church? Do they have eternal life because they read their Bible? Are they saved because they attend church, or their parents told them that church was the nice thing for them to do, and nice people go to church, and it will help their life? Is someone born again because they count your offering or sing in the choir?" He just stood and stared at me. Of course, he never invited me back.

On another occasion, I was invited to speak at a graduation for a small seminary in Southern California. They had 175 graduates that year. They made the mistake of having me minister to the graduating class. After I was through with my address, God spoke and said, "Give them an altar call." I said, "Lord, these people have gone through seminary! They're graduates!" The Lord's response to me was, "Did you not say you would always give an altar call at every meeting?" I obeyed and gave an altar call. Out of 175 graduates, fifteen were born again that day, along with many family and friends that attended the ceremony!

I believe there are a lot of people in our churches that are really not saved. That's probably why there are church splits. It is the reason for gossip, strife, and division in the church. Our church has never had a church split or any major division. You can't hang around us for long without getting saved.

Can you imagine people in your church who are not saved? It is true for all of us; remember the four types of people in our churches: believers, unbelievers, uninformed, and informed (1 Corinthians 14:22-24).

We have a Sabbath service at our church on Saturdays to reach the community we are in, which is the headquarters for the Seventh Day Adventist denomination. One Saturday morning service, a lady asked me if we believed in the Sabbath. She and her husband had gone to church on the Sabbath all their lives and wanted to make sure that we believed in the Sabbath. I said, "Sure we do, but the Sabbath for us is every day." She really didn't understand what I meant but she said, "I agree with that," and went into the service. I gave the altar call that morning, and both she and her husband came forward to get saved.

You don't get saved by attending church your whole life. It is a major misunderstanding within the community of our Christian culture. We assume that just because people attend our churches, like the message, pat the pastor on the back, and give into the offering, they are qualified for entrance into God's kingdom. Jesus made it clear that we "must be born again" (John 3:3).

> When you give an "aggressive altar call," it creates a great impact in the Kingdom of God.

When you give an "aggressive altar call," it creates a great impact in the Kingdom of God.

Aggressive altar calls have literally changed our church, even down to the way we take people from our altar area to the Altar Worker's Room. Praise God, at our last church facility we had to knock out part of a wall to make double doors into our Altar Worker's Room because of the number of people passing through the doors to get saved! It just took too long for them in single file. At our new church building, we set things up so that people can get into the altar room quickly and easily.

A lot of times we think we are doing a good job by saying, "If you need Jesus, we will pray with you," or, "If you're not saved, we will pray with you." When we do this, we make a desperate mistake for which we are accountable to God. We must take our responsibility to lead people to Jesus more seriously. It would seem, at times, that we think that as long as people like us, come to church, bring their tithe, and serve within some part of the church that they are okay with God. Truth be known, we are responsible to God for making sure that every man, woman, and child who comes through our doors is challenged to surrender all of their hearts and lives to Jesus Christ. That is what makes the difference in their lives.

You Can Learn to Give An Aggressive Altar Call

An aggressive altar call only takes about ten to twelve minutes. I cut my preaching down to about thirty-five minutes to accommodate a ten-minute altar call at the end. It's that important to me and must be to you, or it won't work. I am very convinced it is important to God.

We have even had more than one altar call in a service. Have you ever been in a church service where they took up two or even three offerings? One time, we had five altar calls! Each time, more people responded. During another service, out of 2,000, only four responded. After they came up, we all clapped and sent them out to the altar room.

Then the Spirit of the Lord spoke to me and said, "There are more people than that." You can't be afraid of the people. You must be committed to being used God's way. You must be prepared to be a spectacle for God. So I told the congregation, "God just spoke to me that there's more. I don't know what to do. I can't talk you into it." I put my head down and began to weep. I felt like a fool! As I stood there crying, about eight more people came to the altar. Before that morning was over, everyone was astonished, mouths hanging down to the floor, because almost *fifty* people came forward to give their lives to Jesus Christ! Now, that is church! Because the people leave our services pumped up, and they want to come back. The beauty of this is **you can learn to give an aggressive altar call. You can be a soul winner also.**

A friend of mine who had a church in Hemet, California, gave up his church to be a traveling minister and preach in churches across the country. He came to our church one morning and was just sitting in the service when heard me give an altar call. He said to himself: "I want that!"

After that, everywhere I went to preach, I saw him. I soon realized he was following me around, and I asked him "What are you doing? I see you every place I go." He said to me, "Pastor, I just want that anointing." I explained to him that it was not an anointing but an ability he could learn. I taught him what an altar call is and how to do it. About a year later, he invited me to lunch. He shared with me that in the year since he learned to give an aggressive altar call, he had won more people to the Lord than he had in the twenty years he had been pastoring in his church.

It is said that the average church in America wins six to eight people to the Lord per year. Our church now averages between 11,000-13,000 people won to the Lord each year just in the pulpit areas of our church! We don't count the great ministry outside the walls of our church.

An old friend of mine who pastors a large church invited me to speak at his church. We have a friendly and loving competition going on. I love godly challenges, and I have been pushing him about the altar calls. He really has been getting into them lately, so when I came to speak at his church, his whole staff was laughing that I was just going to "rake the comb through the hair" and only get a few people saved. I laughed back and said, "No, it's not going to be that way. We're going to win souls." By the end of his four weekend services, we had 300 salvations. The pastor got really stirred up about it all, and today he is a great soul winner himself.

We cannot afford to perpetuate a watered down "American" gospel. Winning souls must be our priority. Sure, we must preach about all the things that build maturity in the believer. I thank God for all of that. My wife and kids live in God's abundance and blessing because of that. But we don't neglect the souls of the people who fill our pews. Let's use our faith first for souls! Jesus has called us to bring in the harvest.

Anyone can learn how to win a listening and believing audience. We had a well-known minister come and preach at our church. Everyone came early to try to get front row seats to hear this particular minister, and after his message he gave an altar call. To my surprise, only a few people responded. God spoke to me and said, "Would you please give an altar call?" I said "Oh, God please, this is a well-known minister that I respect! I do not want to diminish what he is doing." So I asked the minister, "Sir, I love and respect you, but the Spirit of God spoke to me. Can I give another altar call?" He was such a gentleman; he said, "Absolutely, you go ahead and do it." So I gave an altar call, and twenty-seven more people came forward. I tell you this not to say that I was a better minister, but because I have learned how to give an aggressive altar call. When you learn how to give an altar call, it will change the whole dynamic of your church and ministry.

People Will Respond to an Aggressive Altar Call.

A woman came to me after a church service and said, "Pastor, I'm so excited! My sister got saved today!" I said "Great!" She continued, "You don't understand pastor, my sister lives in Colombia, South America, and she went to Australia for a vacation. On her way back home, she had a free ticket so she came to visit me. I knew she wasn't saved, so I brought her to church, and she got saved." I said, "That is wonderful! I am so excited for you! God bless you!" She continued again, "But pastor, I don't go to your church." I was surprised. She said she had attended another church in a neighboring city for twenty years. She brought her unsaved sister to a place where she knew that she would get saved! That woman may still be on the roll of the other church, but she is in our services twice a week now.

When people see that people are getting saved in your church, they bring their friends, neighbors, and relatives. We now give an aggressive altar call at every service. My wife and all of our associate pastors give aggressive altar calls and win as many people to the Lord as I do. We build into our people that they are all full-time ministers responsible for reaching out to the unsaved at home, on the job, at school, and wherever they go! They bring them to church to get saved. Even better, they get them saved first, and then bring them to church. People testify with tears in their eyes about their relatives and friends who have gotten saved. One man was saved on a Sunday morning and came back for the Sunday night service with a dozen people. All of them got saved at that service!

How to Give An Aggressive Altar Call

Would you extend me the grace to explain how and why I say what I say in an altar call? I will tell you what I say, and explain why I say it. The things that I say, and what I do, I do for a reason.

I start by saying, **"I want to make sure that everyone in this place is right with God, so I need everyone to stay seated.** The reason for this is so you don't disturb the hearing of the people around you. **When you get up, the people around you might be, at that moment, hearing from God, and you just disturbed what God was telling them. That's rude, and you don't want to be rude!"**

I cover a future problem before it happens, so I start with this because people have a tendency to move around and get up. If I don't keep their attention, I won't win souls. I can't allow the lack of spiritual insight on the part of some people to rob souls from His Kingdom.

The next thing I say is, **"I want to ask you a question, and I want you all to answer it. Answer it in your heart. No one will know, but be honest with yourself and God. Your answer says a lot about you and where you're at with God. The Bible says that you should examine yourself to make sure you are okay with God. Here is the question: if you were to walk out of this church, headed toward** your car, and your heart stopped and you died, would you go to heaven or would you go to hell?"

I say all of this is to show the importance of paying attention. The question is such a blunt question with such a harsh word in it (hell), and that it gets people's immediate attention.

I then say, "Just answer the question in your heart. Now, your answer says a lot about yourself. Some of you answered like this: 'Pastor Jim, I think I'm going to heaven.' The problem with that is nowhere in the Bible does it say that you can go to heaven by being a positive thinker. Some of you said, 'I hope I'm going to heaven.' Again, nowhere in the Bible does it say that you can go to heaven if you have great hope. It's not in the Bible. Some of you thought that you're going to heaven because you love God. Nowhere does it say you can get to go to heaven because you love God! Those guys who stole the airplanes and crashed them into the World Trade Center said they loved God, but my Bible says wrong god and wrong way to express his love. My Bible indicates they are in hell and probably took a lot of people with them. Some of you said to yourself, 'I'm going to heaven because I'm a good person.' Again, nowhere in the Bible does it say that because you are good you get to go to heaven. We got that idea from Hollywood movies and not from the Bible."

What I am doing here is breaking down their false ideas of why they think they are going to Heaven. I heard one man say that it's like getting them unsaved mentally before I can get them truly saved spiritually. They think they are saved, and they are not. So I'm overcoming their objections and false thinking in order to get them to Christ.

I continue, *"Jesus says, 'I am the way, the truth, and the life, and no man goes to the Father except by me.' So you can't get to* heaven your way, or my way, or some well-meaning church committee's way but only God's way."

The point here is to get them to see that their ideas or false thinking do not line up with God. They are starting to become open now.

Then I say, "I know what some of you might be thinking. 'My Mom and Dad told me that I was a Christian. In fact, they took me to Catechism Class, or Sunday School Class, or Sabbath School. They put a cross or a Saint Christopher around my neck. They had me christened or baptized as a child. Why, I've always thought of myself as a Christian.' But nowhere in the Bible does it say that if your parents say and do these things you will be a Christian and will go to Heaven. It's not in the Bible! Some of you might say, 'Wait a minute, Pastor Jim. You don't understand. I joined my last church. It was a Christian church, and I was a leader. Why, for fourteen years I sang in the choir.' Could you show me in the Bible where if you join the church or sing in the choir, or are a church leader, then you get to go to heaven? It's not there."

I keep making my point that it's not in the Bible, breaking down their wrong thinking.

Then I say, "Some of you might even say, 'Someone told me that if I know who Jesus is then that makes me a Christian.' But even Satan knows who Jesus is, and he is *not* a Christian. There is a big difference between knowing Him in your head and believing in Him and having Him in your heart. Jesus, who went to the cross so that you could go to heaven, tells us exactly how to get to heaven. In John chapter three, He says that you must be born again. 'Born again' is a statement that rubs some people the wrong way. We have been taught that born again people are weird and fanatical. We see them on TV, and they look strange and act strange. Hollywood has done a good job of making fun of

Jesus' words because most people in American churches don't know what born again really means. I'll tell you. From the beginning to the end of the Bible, God is looking for all of your heart and all of your life. Yes, *all* of your heart and all of your life. You see, it's is an all-or-nothing relationship with Jesus Christ. It always has been, and it always will be all or nothing. I'll prove it to you. In the last book of the Bible, the book of Revelation, Jesus is speaking. He says, 'When I come again I had better find you hot or cold, but if I find you lukewarm I'll vomit you from my mouth.' That's a real blunt statement, seemingly rude, but what He is really saying is this: lukewarm people are not real Christians and are going to be ejected from His Body. They are not going to make it. Wow, what's lukewarm? A little in and a little out, a little up and a little down, a token prayer and occasional church attendance. God is something to you, but He's not *everything*. You're not against God, but you're not wholeheartedly for Him. Some of you need to hear me, because you're just not going to make it if you don't get right with God."

Now I'm ready, and so are they, to get right with God. I feel God has removed their false crutches and their hearts are open. At this point, I feel good because I've done my job.

"If you're going to get right with God and become truly born again, you're going to have to give God all your heart and life. Notice how I say 'give.' He won't steal it or make you do it. He's not a thief or conniver that will talk you out of it. It's your heart and your life. Only you can make that choice. You might ask me, 'How do I give God all my heart and life?' Let's not do it my way or your way. Let's do it God's way. Jesus said, 'If you confess me before men, I'll confess you before my Father.' In a moment I'll count to three and pop my hands together like this." (I say it and pop my hands.)

I do this so they can know when to put up their hands. When I do this and they hear my loud hand clap, it literally wakes them up and brings their attention back to me.

Then I say, "When you hear this sound (I do it again), you put your hand up. By raising your hand, you're saying, 'I don't want to go to hell, and I want to give God all my heart and all my life and be born again."

Now I must overcome the objection of raising their hand. So I say, "I know what some of you are saying to yourself right now. You're saying, 'If I raise my hand, I'll be embarrassed.' You might be, but get over it. After all, it's better to be embarrassed in this safe place for a moment than to be in hell forever and ever and ever. Do you care more about what people think or more about what God sees?"

I've overcome the objection of embarrassment. Then I say, "Who should raise their hand when I pop my hands together?" I pop my hands together again. Now they have heard it three times and know what to do.

"If you've been running from God instead of to Him, I'm talking to you. Get ready to put your hand up. If you have never given God all your heart or never given God all your life, I'm speaking to you. Get ready to put your hand up. If you're not sure, make sure. Get ready to put your hand up. If you prayed with Billy Graham or at a crusade but never followed up with your part of that prayer, then make a wholehearted commitment today. Today is your day of salvation. I'm going to count and clap my hands. Are you ready? One! Two! Three! Bang."

When hands start to go up, I start to count them: "One, two three," etc. The reason for counting is that it builds excitement in the house, and more hands start to go up. I don't let anyone applaud. People are sheep, and they will follow others and clap themselves. They will clap and not raise their hands. So I tell the people, **"Don't scare my fish away by clapping."** I have trained the church not to clap during the altar call. It takes time to train your church. Be patient and explain what you want from them, and they will help you.

After I count the hands, then I say, **"I want all of you that raised your hand to come forward. So get your Bible, sweater, purse, and all of your stuff. If you need to bring a friend, bring your friend. So let's all stand, and if you raised your hand or if you know you should have raised your hand but didn't, you can come also. Let's give them a hand as they come."** As they start to come, our altar workers start to walk up first. Why? Because when people see others coming, they come. Once they all get in front, I introduce them to our pastor over new salvations and I tell them that he is going to do three things. **"First, he will lead you in a prayer to invite Jesus into your heart and life. Second, give you some free stuff that you can take home and read about what you should do next now that you're saved. Third, introduce you to our Spiritual Personal Trainers for future growth."** All of this takes about fifteen minutes, and in order for it to work, you must make time for it to happen. It's worth it because this will change your people's lives, your church, and even your city. It pleases God, and God brings people to church. Lots and lots of people! When you learn to apply these principles, your church will double and triple over and over again.

The question now becomes, "How do you follow up on all of those new believers?" At The Rock, we get the congregation to play their part as "full-time ministers" to mentor or "father" these new converts. It is done on a one-on-one basis, and in our church we call it the SPT program. SPT stands for "Spiritual Personal Trainer." The people who respond and come forward and pray are taken to an

Altar Worker's Room where they are given some brief instruction, some gospel materials to help them in their walk with Jesus, and an SPT of the same approximate age and gender. The SPT's then follow up on these new Christians and meet with them thirty minutes before a church service of their choice for five consecutive weeks. Why five weeks? Because if I can get them back for five weeks, they have now become comfortable in the church and feel as if they belong.

I would love to go into detail regarding discipleship and how to create more "followshippers," not leaders. However, that is outside the scope of this book on Pastoring In His Presence and is a topic I look forward to addressing in a future book.

You now know how I have learned to do an aggressive altar call and why I do it that way, and I pray that you can learn to use this in your church to help many, many people come to a saving knowledge of Jesus Christ.

Sample Salvation Prayer to Use in Your Altar Call

"Everyone Say:

> Father God, I come to you and thank you for Jesus. Today and forever, I believe that Jesus Christ is Your only begotten Son, that You sent Him for me, and that He died for me.
>
> I repent of my sins and receive Jesus as my Lord and Savior, today and forever. My sins are washed away, and I'm free forevermore. Let it be known that today and forever I am saved, washed by His blood, alive, and have the victory of His cross. I'm born again, headed for Heaven, and a child of God. Thank you, Jesus!"

CONCLUSION

It is my greatest desire to hear of how you are building the Kingdom of God, and how your church is becoming a force in your community that will change the very atmosphere of life.

When you become **pleasing**, you can expect His **presence**; from His presence comes His **power**; from His power comes His **anointing**; and it is in His anointing that all things become **"GOOD,"** (remember the tree).

We cannot pastor in the church as CEOs lead in the business world. We must take our direction from God, and then we must follow Him closely. We who are called to be shepherds are not truly leaders in the Body of Christ; we are followers teaching "followship" to those who come behind us.

I hope that my transparency and lessons of failure and success have been a blessing to you, and I look forward to hearing how God can use these hard-won lessons to help your church grow and lead many people to Jesus.

jim@jimcobrae.com

Now, go out and Pastor In His Presence.

PASTOR JIM COBRAE'S BIO

Pastor Jim Cobrae has been preaching the gospel for over forty years. He is the founding pastor of The Rock Church and World Outreach Center located in San Bernardino, California. Pastor Jim is known for his direct approach to the Word of God and his humorous insights into everyday life. He has a passion for soul-winning and discipleship and has seen hundreds of thousands of people give their lives to Christ over the past twenty-nine plus years since The Rock began in 1988. His love for people and commitment to demonstrate the goodness of God has seen a church become a world outreach center locally and globally. He is married to Deborah his partner in life and ministry and has four grown children, all serving the Lord, along with twelve grandkids and one great-grandchild. His desire in the later part of life is to encourage pastors to go way beyond their own expectations.